P9-EGN-292

GELLHORN

on any other kind of civic undertaking, that she did not, in the years to come, occupy. She seems to have been a woman without guile or vanity; energetic and immensely practical; born, as Martha might have said, with the lucky nature that invites a lucky life. As Martha's second husband, Tom Matthews, would observe many years later, when you were with her you somehow felt better not just about yourself but about the whole human race.

When Martha was around twelve, she came home one day from the Mary Institute, the girls' private day school attended by the daughters of St. Louis's professional families, with a new biology textbook. Leafing through it, Dr. Gellhorn was irritated to see in the pictures of the human body that everything below the navel was a blank. It was the spur that he and Edna needed to push for a new school, coeducational and progressive, to match the reforms sweeping through the city's institutions, and in keeping with the progressive school movement in vogue in America. John Burroughs School, named after a well-known naturalist, with a curriculum that included a course on the life of the city, was designed to foster a sense of pride in St. Louis and prevent young people from departing for the East Coast as soon as they could get away. It opened in the autumn of 1923. There was much talk of the "beautiful religion of service," and both boys and girls gardened and played baseball on the eighteen-acre grounds, as the school followed Dewey in maintaining that there was no difference between male and female physiognomy. Martha and Alfred were among its first pupils, paying the then-considerable fees of $1,000 a year. Martha was one of a dozen in the top form. The two children caught the tram, the "special" from near their house, for the fifty-minute ride to the suburbs, and Alfred remembers that Martha, embarrassed by having a little brother, forced him to walk on the other side of the road and not stand too near her. Soon, John Burroughs School had a debating society, a school council, and a magazine; on all of these she took a leading part, becoming Speaker of the assembly and president of the Dramatic Association, saying later that she always wanted to be the leader of anything she became involved in, as she preferred bossing others to being bossed. Following Dr. Gellhorn's house rules, she drafted the new school's constitution, and she contributed to the first issue of the school magazine a review of a collection of Galsworthy's stories, a short story of her own about life in Russia under the czars, and a poem with a mournful refrain:

"Peace! do not mourn the dead,
They're in a happier land," I said
And be a man! (yes, be a man)

But when to me great sorrow came
It seemed the case was not the same
Forsooth, why should I be a man? Why? Why?

In an essay she wrote breezily and with weary sophistication during her sixteenth year, she described the world as a "hypocritical hole, blackened by lies and deceit." But poetry, at this stage, was where she had decided her future lay, and she was fortunate in that John Burroughs School had attracted two exceptional English teachers, one of them the future novelist Stanley Pennell, who both encouraged her writing. Having learned the rewards of boldness from her mother's example, she sent some of her poems to Carl Sandburg, asking for his opinion. He must, she wrote later, have been not only a wise man but a nice one. The poems came back with a short handwritten note. "If you must be a writer," Sandburg had scrawled, resorting to a safe Delphic utterance, "you will be." When she wasn't writing, Martha read, mainly books belonging to her father, like Knut Hamsun's three-volume *Growth of the Soil,* which Dr. Gellhorn kept in the bathroom, or a collection of horror stories, found in her brother Walter's room.

As the children grew up, family life began to be marked by quarrels between George Gellhorn and his eldest son. The young George was restless and unpredictable, irked by his father's ambitions for him. At sixteen, perhaps to general relief, he left home for Annapolis, from where he joined the navy, and seldom came home again. Walter, more pliant and bookish than his older brother, got on better with his father, but neither felt much affection for the other. Walter went off to college at Amherst, then on to what was to become an outstanding law career. Alfred was his father's natural heir. On Sundays, Dr. Gellhorn took the young boy with him on his rounds of black patients, pausing at one of the city's museums on the way home to show him a single object of beauty or interest. Alfred loved his parents' company. Having been persuaded by Walter to follow his father into medicine, he chose to pursue his medical studies in St. Louis, in order to live at home.

When Alfred was twelve, and Martha seventeen, George Gellhorn decided that the moment had come to show his two younger children his native Germany. They rented a red Mercedes-Benz and drove to Breslau and Würzburg. She and Alfred, Martha wrote later, behaved like "barbarians." Alfred only wanted to swim or to eat. Martha, by now interested in young men, "mooned around, looking at everything but not inquiring as to what she might be seeing." At the Alte Pinakotek in Munich, she announced that Rubens made her feel sick; at the Bayreuth Festival, she said that she loathed opera. The Germans she found "shockingly ugly." "My father," she wrote, "struggled bitterly, despairingly and heroically against us." Having longed for "wakeful, interested and original minds," he was forced to conclude that his children were "lumpish." For her part, Martha would complain that her father was a perfectionist, setting for himself and others the sternest standards. She knew the drawbacks of perfectionism all too well, for what he termed *divine dissatisfaction* was something that she shared. Writing later to a friend, she confessed that she had a great deal of her father's blood in her, and "he was a man who used to inform people that their doorbells were broken, and run his finger thoughtfully if silently over dirty surfaces and also look at people with friendly interest, as though they were under microscopes, and tell them they looked as if they drank/ate, or whatever, too much." For her mother, who loved, admired, and encouraged all her children, whatever they did, Martha felt lifelong love; but it was really her father, she would say, who taught her about justice, independent thought, and compassion. He gave her the gift of curiosity and a taste for excellence.

With suffrage had come domestic freedoms of a kind American women had not experienced before the war. Even if there was no sudden rush of young women into offices and public life, the drudgery of housekeeping had been agreeably diminished by the arrival of canned food, commercial laundries, and inventions like vacuum cleaners. Magazines and popular books in the early 1920s portrayed men and women dancing cheek to cheek or sitting together in speakeasies, drinking the fashionable new cocktails. There was a vogue for wearing rouge and powdering your face in public, and the fashion for straight, long-waisted dresses included skirt lengths that rose steadily season by season toward the knee. Manufacturers concentrated on finding new admired his speech. Briand invited her to dinner. The evening went well and she enjoyed his fatherly manner and his indiscreet gossip about fellow delegates, but she had expected sonorous pronouncements about the state of the world, and a certain weariness from bearing the weight of international peace on his shoulders. It gave her a first glimpse of the ordinariness of leaders and of the way that power seemed to have so little to do with inspiration, and she never forgot it.

Afterward she walked around the city, eating hot cheese rolls and hoping that Briand had, at the very least, a good heart. Then she went to look for the other foreign correspondents, who sat together drinking between sessions in the Café Lutetia, and was extremely pleased to note that this illustrious group seemed perfectly willing to accept her as one of their own. She was getting a first taste of that particular excitement that all journalists experience, when they suddenly feel they have understood a complicated story, perceived its underlying truths, and become party to its innermost secrets. "I believed," she wrote, "that if everyone knew the truth, justice would be done."

After Geneva, Bertrand took Martha to Italy in November. He had left Marcelle and now, whenever parted from Martha, wrote her loving letters. "My beloved, I am so happy—We have such a marvellous life— Your work—my work—our car—our Sundays—our nights—our friends—We're independent—we're free—we're proud—we're young— we're in love—we stand out from all others. . . . Oh my love." He called her Rabbit. She called him Smuf. They traveled down the coast to Rapallo, then back up again to Tuscany. Under Mussolini's disastrous economic policies industrial production was falling rapidly, and there were said to be huge parts of Italy where children were barely kept alive on tomatoes, bread, and olive oil. But what Martha would chiefly remember about the journey was the day in Florence when they had been planning their future and a telegram came from Marcelle announcing that she was pregnant, and begging Bertrand to return home. What Bertrand would remember was that Martha seemed little interested in her surroundings and preferred to sit in cafés.

Compared with her new friends, well versed in the complexities of modern European politics and culture, Martha felt herself to be extremely ill educated. Knowing the pleasure that it would give her father, and encouraged by Bertrand, who, after a brief spell staying with Marcelle, was again back with her, Martha enrolled at the Haute École des Sciences Politiques on their return to Paris. Remembering her enjoyment of Nietzsche, during her walks in the south of France, she chose to study the German philosophers. It took her barely a couple of weeks to realize her mistake. It was not that she had trouble with either the French or the German language; it was the content of the classes that baffled her. She sat impatiently through a number of lectures, listening to sentences that had no meaning for her; before the end of term she left, saying she would attend political meetings, of which Paris was full, instead. Debate and analysis—neither appealed to her in the way that people did, and how they lived.

Yet her uneasiness about her new life had increased over the months. Her early friends, scruffy, eager, tentative like herself, had scattered and been replaced by Parisians, well-informed, highly politicized people who were at the same time chic and confident. She felt that her clothes were wrong. More and more, she had the uncomfortable feeling that things were expected of her that she had no idea how to deliver. Bertrand was clear about his desire for her, his "wild will to possess." "I have learned," he wrote, "to coat it with light laughter and playfulness. But it's brutal, it's carnal, it's damn real." To Martha, it felt all too real. "I was stuck," she would write later, "with a lot of maddening emotional problems which I did not want. I began to feel like a plaything of destiny which made me at once gloomy, angry and confused." Sometime toward the end of the year, she realized that she, too, was pregnant.

There was no question of marriage, Marcelle having made it clear that she would not give Bertrand a divorce; in any case she wanted him back. Though an abortion would have been easy to fix in Paris— France in the 1930s had the highest number of abortions in Europe— Martha felt "in every way trapped." After Christmas, she booked herself a cheap passage on a ship going to America. She had been in France for ten months. "I knew myself to be old and failed," she wrote with the sense of drama and tragedy that she sometimes went in for during these early years. "My life had come to nothing, I did not have whatever it took to live." Instinctively shrewd about herself, which often made her appear older and wiser on paper than in her behavior, she concluded that it was all due to a constant need for heroes. "Despite my best efforts to turn everyone I met into a hero, people sensibly enough did not feel like playing the part thrust on them. . . . Since others would not perform as I demanded or expected, I had to do it myself and act heroically." Bertrand had failed to live up to her ideal.

THREE

A LITTLE HUNGRY
FOR A LONG TIME

MARTHA'S DIARY FOR December 1930 consists of one short entry. "Xmas (?)," it says. "St. Louis (ill and pregnant)." Dr. Gellhorn was evidently angry and unforgiving about his daughter's involvement with the married Bertrand; at some point, he called her "selfish scum." In January, she went to Chicago for an abortion. Martha wrote nothing about it, neither then nor later. In keeping with her self-imposed stoicism and with her refusal to allow herself to complain, she seems to have treated the loss of Bertrand's child in her customary brisk, matter-of-fact way. It had to be done; the thing was to do it efficiently, quickly, and with the minimum of fuss. Anything else would have been unacceptably self-indulgent. One can only speculate about what this may have cost her in terms of real pain, grief stored up and not allowed to surface.

In America, as in France, society was at a moment of rapid and confusing change. The Coolidge prosperity under which she had grown up had seen young women for the first time earn decent salaries, move around freely and unchaperoned, and live in flats on their own. She had read *The Great Gatsby* and *Babbitt* and the new literary magazines, like *American Mercury*, that were published in the 1920s, and laughed with H. L. Mencken at sentimentality and academic pomposity. "I rebelled naturally," she later observed. "I understood experimenting: my whole life has been an experiment." With Einstein, Freud, and Bertrand Russell had come the heady new thought that not only was there no such thing as unquestionable right or wrong, but that certainty of any kind was an illusion. And even if the Wall Street crash of October 1929 had returned a measure of formality and conservatism to American life, the Gellhorns personally had been little hit by the financial upheavals. There was a family story that Dr. Gellhorn had once acquired some stock on a friend's advice, but having forgotten its name, spent hours at the breakfast table with his children trying to guess which one it was.

As part of their liberal tradition, the Gellhorns had brought up their only daughter with clear views about tolerance, censorship, and racial and sexual equality, and certain immutable standards of personal behavior. Onto these, while with Bertrand in Paris, she had grafted a new and less rigid morality, one that involved few obligations, beyond that of listening to one's own instincts and desires. Bertrand saw their love affair as excitingly bound up with the freedoms of postwar Europe; Dr. Gellhorn saw it as painfully self-centered and ultimately destructive. Martha herself lay uneasily somewhere in the middle, genuinely convinced that she was applying their standards to her own life, yet believing that what she and Bertrand had together should not be sacrificed to respectability. She craved her parents' approval, but neither she nor her father were prepared to make concessions. "My mother," Martha wrote later, "loved us both and was miserable for us both." But even Edna, who was "much smarter than anyone I know," did not seem to sympathize with her conflict of loyalties. "I think I am probably sexually repressed and all queer because I have scrambled sex and aesthetics and morals and fear into a stinking mess and I'm suffocating somewhere at the centre," she wrote to a friend, evidently struggling to sort out the contradiction she felt between her very obvious attractiveness to men and her own lack of responsive feelings.

Once again, she was rescued by work. For the next four months, living on somewhat strained terms at home, she filled her days with her novel, and with short stories and articles, of which she would produce dozens of fragments, all neatly typed, in the next few years. Some were written in the first person; some were set in America, others in Paris; many revolved around the lives of cub reporters, young women writers, their parents and brothers and sisters, and the tensions between them, or around friendships between older and younger women. There are ones about abortions and about college life. The tone is often a little lofty. The heroines, dark haired and silent, have "infinitely languid" eyes. "I wrote as I breathed and saw," Martha would later note in a diary, "very fast, not worrying, it was as easy as a worm's digestion. I swallowed the world around me and it came out in words." There was not a great deal of room for feelings.

None of these stories appear to have been published, and it is possible that none were even submitted for publication. But it was not in Martha's nature to brood. Sometime in April 1931, deciding that she needed a break from St. Louis, she persuaded the *Post-Dispatch* to pay her twenty-five dollars for every story it took for its Sunday magazine, and the Missouri Pacific Railway to give her a free Pullman pass in exchange for publicizing its routes to the west. Alone, a roving correspondent in a "brand new outfit" of a blue cotton shirt and full skirt, with sneakers on her feet and a small suitcase she decided more suitable to her new role than a knapsack, she "bounced across the continent to the Pacific coast and back . . . and America looked vast, beautiful and empty." She paused in Texas, Nevada, New Mexico, and California, interviewed a woman bullfighter named Juanita, and sought out three of her heroes, Tom Mooney, the imprisoned union leader, the heavyweight boxer Jack Dempsey, and the poet Robinson Jeffers, whose message about man's egocentricity and indifference to the beauties of nature had struck her keenly. All three made for "flashy prose" soon speeding its way back to the *Post-Dispatch*. The first story to appear was about a town in East Texas, where a sudden discovery of oil had brought "human bedlam . . . a forest of oil wells, towers eighty feet high . . . machinery scraping, chugging, pounding," and where the three Texas Rangers in charge of law and order kept their drunken prisoners chained by the leg to a peg in a circle of dust. "The gaunt new millionaires," wrote Martha, "sat in rocking chairs on their crumbling porches, bemused," their fingers thickly covered in diamond rings. At night, she slept in a derailed Pullman car, eating cold baked beans out of the can, watching the oil men gamble "while greenbacks fluttered down like falling leaves." They addressed her as "little lady" and apologized for their bad language.

In Reno, "land of the lotus eaters," she wrote about "women with indiscriminate hips, clothes by Sears Roebuck, speakeasies serving dago red called sparkling burgundy," and complained that never before had his family sink into misery. At what point did he simply give up and become "downhearted and brooding and dangerous"? Only then did Hopkins think he would truly be able to take the pulse of the nation and devise a sound relief program for the "third of the nation" that was "ill-nourished, ill-clad, ill-housed."

To know just what impoverished, unemployed America was feeling, to construct what was essentially a vast demographic portrait of the Great Depression, Hopkins turned to the statistics on rural poverty that flooded into his office in Washington from Oregon and Colorado, Utah and North Dakota, Illinois and Massachusetts. His rural research supervisors analyzed data; his statisticians collated figures; and his case-workers put together family profiles. He was deluged by facts. But Hopkins wanted something more, something more intangible and descriptive.

And so, in the summer of 1933, he hired an erratic, tough, forty-one-year-old newspaper reporter named Lorena Hickok, who smoked a pipe and had a rasping cough, and had once been described by a colleague as a "big girl in a casual raincoat with a wide tailored hat, translucent blue eyes, and a mouth vivid with lipstick." She was built, said Martha, like a tank and weighed almost 200 pounds, and she played poker and drank bourbon with the boys. The daughter of a butter maker from Wisconsin, Lorena Hickok was a close friend of Eleanor Roosevelt's, having covered her side of the election campaign for a series of articles and declared herself much impressed by her good sense, humor, and determination. Hopkins gave her the title of chief investigator and sent her off to tell him what she saw and heard, while never for a moment forgetting "that but for the grace of God, you, I, and any of our friends might be in their shoes."

Over the next twelve months Lorena Hickok visited every part of the country except the Northwest, mostly by bus, but then, once she had learned to drive, in a battered old Chevrolet, banging and rattling her way across the immense distances of America, stopping to talk to farmers and teachers, officials and housewives, factory workers and policemen, children, blacks, Hispanics, the sick, the elderly. The letters she sent back to Hopkins were breezy, irreverent, and engaging. Late at night, using capital letters for emphasis, she wrote about the "gaunt, ragged legion of the industrially damned. Bewildered, apathetic, many of them terrifyingly patient."

Hickok's reports soon convinced Hopkins that he was right in his hunch that this was the way to learn things about the depression that no amount of facts would ever teach him. He started to recruit other newspaper reporters, novelists, and writers, people accustomed to listening to what people said and writing it all down simply and clearly. While Hickok had all America as her beat, the newcomers were assigned either a region or a major city and its immediate surroundings.

There was Louisa Wilson, daughter of a missionary to China, a star Washington profile writer, whose girlish clothes and manner concealed ambition and determination; Wilson was assigned to the automobile centers of Detroit and Michigan, and to Ohio. There was Ernestine Ball, the reporter known for her series of articles about Aimee Semple McPherson, the religious revivalist. She was given upstate New York. Wayne Parrish, a Pulitzer Prize winner and traveling scholar with a passion for aeronautical engineering, got New York itself. David Maynard, one of the two economists on the team, who had worked for the League of Nations, was allocated the midwestern industrial towns of Cleveland, Cincinnati, and Indianapolis. And Martha, at twenty-five one of the youngest of the investigators, and their sixteenth member, was dispatched to the textile areas of the Carolinas and New England. Their instructions were all the same: go to wherever unemployment and poverty are to be found; talk to everyone you see; write down what they tell you and what your impressions are; and send it in. Their pay was thirty-five dollars a week. Those who had cars took them. The others, like Martha, cadged lifts from local FERA social workers or caught buses, trains, and trolleys. Sometimes they went on foot. What they came back with was a haunting picture of despair.

It was in the textile mill towns of North Carolina that Martha finally found the writing voice that she had been looking for. It was clear and very simple, a careful selection of scenes and quotes, set down plainly and without hyperbole. Nothing particularly distinctive, there were many other writers who did the same, some just as well. What made it her own was the tone, the barely contained fury and indignation at the injustice of fate and man against the poor, the weak, the dispossessed. Nothing so enraged her as bullying, superiority, the misuse of power; nothing touched her so sharply as people who had become victims, through the stupidity or casual brutality of others, or children who were frightened, in pain, or who did not have enough to eat. In Gastonia, among those who had lost everything, she at last had her subject. For the next sixty years, in wars, in slums, in refugee camps, she used this voice again and again, handling it with such a sure ear for nuance that only very rarely did she stray over that fine line into the mawkish or shrill. Unmistakably, it became her hallmark.

Before leaving Washington, Martha was given vouchers for her trains to the South and five dollars a day for food, hotels, and local travel. Broke as ever, she had no money with which to buy sensible clothes and stout shoes suited to tramping around derelict towns in the late autumn. So she went with what she had, which happened to be the discarded dresses and tailor-made suits from Parisian couturiers, once worn by models in the collections. She reached her first destination, Gaston County in North Carolina, "flat and grim as can be expected," in a Schiaparelli suit, with a high Chinese collar fastened by large brown leather clips, and on her head a brown crochet hat out of which rose a brightly colored plume of cock pheasant feathers. Her face was thickly made up, with plenty of mascara, eye shadow, and lipstick. It says much for her complete disregard for the effect she made on others that no one seems to have held her flamboyant appearance against her, and that it took her some time to realize that her turnout was odd.

Martha had a knack for total absorption in work. Soon, she was engrossed by what she was doing, interviewing up to five families a day among the thousands of mill hands and sharecroppers scrounging for jobs that no longer existed, along with factory owners, doctors, union representatives, teachers, and relief workers. Meticulously, she noted rates of pay, levels of relief, and the story of each family. She trudged around slums of tumbledown shacks in her elegant Parisian shoes, where latrines drained into the well from which all drinking water came; she looked at "houses shot with holes, windows broken, no sewerage, rats"; she listened to children so listless with malnutrition that they could barely stay awake, trying to recite the Gettysburg Address for her by heart; she heard doctors talk about rickets, hookworm, anemia, and pellagra, the skin disease of the starving, caused by vitamin deficiency, and the starving, and the way that it had become endemic after months on a diet of pinto beans and corn bread, and about tuberculosis, which was spreading fast through the villages. In one factory, she found three young women lying on the bathroom floor, their eyes closed; they told her they had come in to rest for a few minutes because the eight-hour shifts on heavy machines with no breaks was making them faint. And as she traveled around, her indignation rose, and her reports began to include more observations and conclusions of her own, more recommendations for action, in tones of outrage that grew ever more precise and icy. A doctor, she wrote, had told her that his patients were "degenerating" before his eyes. "The present generation of unemployed," she went on, "will be useless human material in no time. Their housing is frightful (talk about European slums); they are ignorant and often below-par intelligence." Returning from a mill town where those fortunate enough still to have jobs were forced to pay half as much again for their food at the company store, she added: "It is probable—and to be hoped—that one day the owners of this place will get shot and lynched." The people who really touched her were those who, too proud to go on relief, unable to understand why their entire lives had collapsed around them, were desperately hanging on with occasional part-time work, while their children slowly starved to death. This was an America Martha did not know. The flappers and cocktails and mah-jongg parties popularized by F. Scott Fitzgerald and the fashion magazines had not filtered below the top levels of society. Country roads were seldom paved and were often unpassable in snow or heavy rain. It was another world.

Everywhere she went, in the first few weeks, Martha found cases of syphilis. In one town a doctor told her that it had reached the level of an epidemic, and that unless the government decided to treat it as an emergency, as with smallpox, there was no way to halt it. She saw twelve-year-old girls with open syphilitic sores, a baby paralyzed by it, syphilitic families sleeping four to a bed. She discovered that while the blacks referred to it as "rheumatism," the whites called it "bad blood." And as she went from one sick family to the next, with "morons" in every generation, and a new baby every year, she began to write back to Hopkins about the need for birth control, urging him to explore ways of breaking this nightmarish cycle of sickness and overcrowding. "Birth control is needed here almost more than in any other area I have seen," she wrote from North Carolina. "There is one village where half the population is pathologic, and reproducing half wits with alarming vigor." Like syphilis, mental retardation began to obsess her. "Another bright thought: feeblemindedness is on the increase. . . . Out of every three families I visited one had moronic children or one moronic parent. I don't mean merely stupid, I mean . . . fit only for sanitariums."

Like Hopkins, Martha carried in her mind a vision of a strong and purposeful America, seeing behind the daily scenes of malnutrition and apathy the collapse of the great American dream. The "foreign born," or first-generation Americans, she noted, still proud of their few possessions, were standing up better to the depression than the "natives," whose "homes were quickly going to hell" under filth, decay, and demoralization. She reported being told by social workers that the unemployed on relief were becoming entirely dependent not only on the dole itself but on the people who handed it out. And yet, she added, "with all this, they are a grand people. If there is any meaning in the phrase 'American stock' it has some meaning here. They are sound and good humoured; kind and loyal. I don't believe they are lazy; I believe they are mostly ill and ignorant. . . . It is a terribly frightening picture."

If this was what Hopkins had suspected and feared, Martha's next reports touched on far more sensitive matters. On November 5 she reached Boston, and for the next ten days she traveled around Massachusetts, worrying that, by moving so quickly, she was sending only a "bird's eye view," and from a bird flying high and fast at that. On the twenty-fifth, she sat down to her report. The picture, she began, "is so grim that whatever words I use will seem hysterical and exaggerated." All the families she had seen were in the same condition: "[of] fear—fear driving them into a state of semi-collapse; cracking nerves; and an overpowering terror of the future. . . . I haven't been in one house that hasn't offered me the spectacle of a human being driven beyond his or her powers of endurance and sanity. . . . It is hard to believe that these conditions exist in a civilised country." There was more. It was not only the poverty that was at fault: it was the administration of relief itself. In writing about the state of affairs in Massachusetts, Martha abandoned all efforts at restraint. "It is impossible," she wrote, "travelling through this state and seeing our relief set up not to feel that here incompetence has become a menace. . . . It is a bum business from every point of view. . . . The Public Welfare very probably gets the laurel for low type human animal in this job. . . .

Politics is bad enough in any shape; but it shouldn't get around to manhandling the destitute." The greed and stupidity of those in power: already, for Martha, a picture of the world was being formed. It looked to her very bleak.

At the beginning of December, Martha reached Providence, Rhode Island, and found a hotel. Her spirits had never been so low, and though she got dressed in the morning, she spent the "dark" day lying on her bed, "numb and doubting." In a long letter to Bertrand, written on the portable typewriter she carried everywhere with her, she talked about the modern world as a disordered and final battle for the survival of the fittest, in which there was little to tell between the vulgar, narrow, and priggish ruling class, and the 50 percent who were unemployed. "I thank God," she wrote, "I have no children and I want none. This mess is unworthy of new life. As for me: I am ill—principally from nerves, and because my brain is rushing in unhealthy circles. . . . And very sick at heart; and very alone. Another myth: America is beautiful. Oh Christ what a thought. It's ugly, horribly ugly; raw and unkempt; nasty, littered, awkward. The trees don't grow tall enough and the land is torn and dishevelled. It moves endlessly ahead, without shape or grace; and over it are spread the haphazard homes of a shifting, unrooted, grey people. . . .

"Gawd, you can see I'm low. . . . I have no one here to talk to— think of it, 120,000,000 people; and the rabbit hasn't found a pal. Well, well, no doubt there's something wrong with the rabbit."

Alone, despondent, and angry, Martha decided that she had seen enough. She returned to Washington and, according to her own account, stormed into Hopkins's office and harangued him about the way relief was being administered, before giving her notice, adding that she had plans to write and expose what she had witnessed. By all reports, Hopkins was a calm and sensible man. He told her that he had sent her reports to Mrs. Roosevelt; why didn't she discuss it all with her? Edna Gellhorn and Eleanor Roosevelt had become friends while Edna was at Bryn Mawr, and Martha had grown up to admire her selfless campaigning. Invited to dinner at the White House, she grudgingly accepted. When she got there, she was outraged at the apparent luxury, and particularly at the gold-and-white china.

Mrs. Roosevelt was a little deaf. A terrible moment came when she rose from her place at the long dining room table and shouted down to her husband at the other end, her voice high and patrician like her husband's. "Franklin, talk to that girl. She says all the unemployed have pellagra and syphilis." There was silence; then an explosion of laughter. The president, trying not to smile, listened politely while Martha, more angry than embarrassed, talked about her travels through the mill towns. He asked her to come back and tell him more. And when, not long afterward, Mrs. Roosevelt persuaded her that she could do far more for the unemployed by sticking to her job, it marked the beginning of a close friendship, one of the most devoted attachments of her life. "She gave off light," Martha would write many years later. "I cannot explain it better."

What Mad Pursuit had at last appeared in 1934, the publisher, Frederick A. Stokes, having accepted Martha's reluctant last round of cuts. Even so, her world-weary story of three college girls in search of something to believe in, and their brushes with syphilis, adultery, and drink, caused a not altogether flattering stir among reviewers, though the *St. Louis Post-Dispatch* listed her name among those of outstanding local women, together with Betty Grable. The *Buffalo Evening News* called her heroines "hectic," and most newspapers drew attention to her respectable St. Louis origins, her elegance, and the fact that she had married the marquis de Jouvenel. Edna was quoted as saying that her daughter was a "knight without armour" and never afraid of the truth and, somewhat more disconcertingly, that she was already "writing much better." The most perceptive review appeared in the *New York Times*. "Crude as it is, there is something fresh and appealing about this book. It would be more likable if Miss Gellhorn were not so enamored of her own heroine, and if she did not dabble so ineffectually with questions of social justice. . . . If she does not go to Hollywood, as she easily might, she may do good work." Martha had no intention of going to Hollywood, but she minded the reviews and the poor sales, though she dismissed the reviewers sharply as "immature and unreasonable." "When I think of what went into making the book, and see how little it counts, I am dismayed before the future," she wrote to Bertrand.

What Mad Pursuit, "palpable juvenilia" as a reviewer noted, was consigned to a closed past: Martha never listed it among the things she wrote, and made sure that once it went out of print, it stayed there. It

Underwear Company. And at the end of February, feeling as if she were at last emerging from a long period in prison or Siberia—and in a "great hurry to be . . . in any sort of trouble I can find anywhere"— she set off for New York, Hemingway having begged her to get there before he left.

New York with Hemingway was not what she had expected. In Key West there had been time for long flirtatious meetings, time to talk seductively about writing and political commitments. In New York they were always in a crowd, everyone drinking, rushing in and out, answering the telephone, going to the Stork Club and Twenty One. "Oh it was very dashing—and vulgar." She was frantic herself. She needed papers for Spain and with some difficulty eventually persuaded her friend Kyle Crichton at *Collier's* magazine to give her not exactly a job but a letter identifying her as its special correspondent. *Collier's,* an early critic of Prohibition, was a loyal supporter of Roosevelt and the New Deal, and its editor in chief, Bill Chenery, a distinguished stiff-necked Virginian, and its editor, Charles Colebaugh, a short and stocky Scot, were both men who set great store by good writing. The success of the magazine, currently more than holding its own against the older, stodgier *Saturday Evening Post,* showed how keen the public was becoming for more liberal and wide-ranging magazines.

Martha also needed money for her boat ticket to Europe. *Vogue* obligingly commissioned her to write an article on the "Beauty Problems of the Middle-Aged Woman"—Martha was not yet twenty-eight—which involved acting as a guinea pig for a new experimental skin treatment, the skin peeled away chemically, leaving fresh layers underneath. (It ruined her skin, she told her friend Diana Cooper many years later, but it got her to Spain.) Someday, she told a friend, "I shall be a great writer and stick to misery which is my province and limit my reforming to the spirit and the hell with the flesh."

There was nothing now to keep her. Before boarding her ship, she wrote to Mrs. Barnes, a family friend in St. Louis: "Me, I am going to Spain with the boys. I don't know who the boys are, but I am going with them."

When the Popular Front Coalition, promising widespread reform, had assumed power in February 1936, Spain was a vast, backward country where people still believed in witchcraft, and wealthy landowners, a corrupt and lazy bureaucracy, and an immensely powerful church ruled with the help of the Guardia Civil, men who wore tricorn hats and tall polished boots. There were few paved roads. Priests, who were often feared and hated, regarded universal literacy as dangerous and had been known to stop children from learning to read lest they be corrupted by modern progressive ideas. Spain was also a country exceptionally given to political passion, from the anti-Semitism of the extreme Nationalists to the puritanism of the anarchists, who held that all measures were legitimate in the struggle to free Spain from fascism. There were dozens of political parties, whose initials varied from place to place, and whose positions shifted from month to month.

Less than half the country had actually voted for the new republic. The new prime minister, Manuel Azaña, was hampered by regional calls for autonomy by the Catalans and the Basques, by violent anti-clericalism, which had already led to several atrocities committed against priests, nuns, and churches, and by a communist-led uprising of miners in the Asturias. By the summer of 1936, strikes, clashes, and random violence had erupted into full-scale fighting, bringing the youngest European general since Napoleon, Francisco Franco, to the head of the Nationalist force, which was now fighting its way across Spain, committing atrocities as it went. Though the Loyalist forces of the republic committed atrocities of their own, Léon Jouhaux, the French trade unionist, coined the memorable phrase of a struggle "of the light against the night," and many people were soon repeating it. Spain became the place in which one talked in opposites: fascists against democrats, religion against atheism, the rich against the poor, bosses against workers. For Loyalists and Nationalists alike, the civil war was a crusade, and even as André Malraux, Martha's hero and the author of the Prix Goncourt–winning *La Condition humaine*, was prophesying that fascism would spread "its great black wings over Europe," not just Spaniards but people all over the world began to project their own hopes and fears onto a conflict that grew more divisive and murderous day by day.

By the end of July 1936, the Nationalists had taken Burgos, Segovia, Avila, Saragossa, Teruel, Pamplona, all of Navarre, and much of Estremadura, their experienced troops facing untrained, disorganized men equipped with primitive weapons and led by ordinary soldiers in the ranks, most military officers having joined the rebels. On August 14, the Nationalists took Badajoz, on the frontier with Portugal, herded all the men they suspected of fighting against them into the bullring, and opened fire with machine guns. Eighteen hundred bodies were counted; the blood, according to Jay Allen of the *Chicago Tribune,* flowed as deep as a man's palm. By the end of September, they had taken Toledo and were pushing on toward Madrid.

Once it had become clear that, for all their military victories, they faced courageous and determined opponents, the Nationalists had appealed to Hitler and Mussolini for weapons and equipment. Supplies poured in. The Germans sent their famous Condor Legion and airlifted Franco's Army of Africa to mainland Spain in Junkers—the first major airlift of troops in military history—while Mussolini, building on his recent triumphs in Abyssinia, sent soldiers, ostensibly "volunteers," as well as airplanes, pilots, and tanks. For their part, the European democracies stood by and did little. When the democratically elected legal republican government begged them for supplies, they drew up a nonintervention pact. One hundred twenty-seven countries agreed to remain "neutral," a pact neither fascist Italy nor Nazi Germany made any pretense of honoring. Stalin, having at first joined the pact, later announced that he would sell weapons to the republic, in return for substantial amounts of Spanish gold. (It was only well over half a century later, when the Russian State Military Archives were finally opened, that the extent to which Stalin shortchanged and double-crossed the republic, effectively swindling it out of several hundred million dollars in arms deals through the secret cooking of accounts, became clear. As did the manner in which the Soviets sent in secret police and military intelligence, setting up a network of secret prisons, in which they tortured and murdered those they considered hostile to communism.)

And as the fighting spread, so foreign volunteers—whether refugees from Hitler or Mussolini, or idealists, or democrats, or left-wing sympathizers, or simply those who, like Martha and Hemingway, saw in Spain a prologue to another world war—arrived in Spain to stand beside the republicans. By early November, when a concerted attack on Madrid by rebel troops began, and the government fled to Valencia, the Moscow-based Comintern helped organize these foreigners—many of whom had never held a gun before—into the International Brigades.

By the end of March 1937, when Martha prepared to leave Paris after a few weeks for the Spanish border, republican morale was perhaps at its highest in the entire war. Four Italian divisions supporting Franco had taken part in a third attempt to encircle Madrid, and had been overwhelmingly routed at the Battle of Guadalajara, northeast of the city, in part due to the tenacity of a battalion of Italian antifascists, the Garibaldi, who had outmaneuvered and outfought Mussolini's fabled Black Flame division. For a moment, it looked as if the republican fortunes could still turn. Madrid, for the time being at least, was safe.

The Poles and the French, the Germans and the Swedes, the Americans and the Greeks—fifty nationalities in all, some 40,000 men, the youngest seventeen, the eldest sixty, and a few women, like Simone Weil—came to fight in the International Brigades on the republican side because the Spanish war brought to the surface all the complex political philosophies and humanitarian dreams of a generation sick of slaughter and conscious of the need for a fairer world. In their wake, throughout 1936 and 1937, came writers, poets, journalists, and a few artists, drawn, like the volunteer soldiers, by a belief in civil rights and democratic government and universal literacy. They came because they had witnessed for themselves what the Nazis were capable of and were appalled, because they sensed that this was probably the last chance to halt the slide toward a full European war, and because Spain represented something in human values that seemed lacking in their own world. "Our spirit," wrote Louis MacNiece, "would find its frontier on the Spanish front / Its body in a rag-tag army." To go to Spain was to be present at the birth of a new and better social order. The burning of books by the Nazis in 1933, and the exodus of writers from Germany and Italy, only confirmed to them that art could not flourish in a reactionary atmosphere, a feeling expressed by many of the writers canvased in 1937 by Nancy Cunard for a symposium on the Spanish civil war in the *Left Review*. As Hemingway would soon tell the Congress of American Writers in New York, "There is only one form of government that cannot produce good writing, and that system is fascism."

Very few of those questioned by the *Left Review*, and very few of those who actually went to Spain, supported the rebels, though writers like Santayana, Ezra Pound, and Paul Claudel hoped that if the republicans were defeated, this would mean the destruction of the menace of communism. Many Catholics, though repelled by Franco's desire to rid Spain of "heretics," agonized over the killing of priests and the burning and desecration of the churches. Most of the 1930s intellectuals, particularly after Spain's great poet, García Lorca, was executed by the Nationalists, shared Léon Jouhaux's image of a struggle between light and dark, and agreed with C. Day-Lewis that Spain was about freedom made "In the image of simple men who have no taste for carnage / But sooner kill and are killed than see the image betrayed." Fascism was unreason, the denial of light.

For many, it was exhilarating to have found a cause, a direction in a decade of chaos and uncertainty, and they never forgot it. "I know, as surely as I know anything in this world," Herbert Matthews, the American reporter, would write after the war was over, "that nothing so wonderful will ever happen to me again as those two and a half years I spent in Spain. . . . It gave meaning to life." Bertrand de Jouvenel, in an elegiac letter to Martha shortly after his own visit to the war, wrote: "I've been happy: the hunger, the thirst, the fatigue, the fear, the horror, all of it was one grand tragedy and I felt alive and I loved all the actors, those who killed and those who were killed. . . . The time for civil wars has come. For wars where at least you know whom you are killing. Rabbit, you will think I have gone off my head. . . . But ah if you'd marched with the Legion, shooting, burning, looting and raping. Darling you would have thought it fine . . . that intensity of feeling one develops in the war I experienced sometimes with you, *quand je t'aimais à fond de train.*" And if much of the vast literature to emerge from the Spanish civil war was indeed sensational in language, sentimental, and too polemical, novels like Malraux's *L'Espoir,* and the personal narratives of Koestler, Bernanos, and Orwell, written later with full knowledge of the treachery, betrayals, and atrocities, did reflect the real complexity of the issues.

But all that came later. For the moment, it was enough to be there, to witness, to write. "We knew, we just *knew* that Spain was the place to stop Fascism," Martha told Phillip Knightley, many years later. "It was one of those moments in history when there was no doubt." One interesting question for Martha, Hemingway, Matthews, and others was how far "all that objectivity shit"—a phrase she surely coined during that war—would actually make it impossible, for writers who had been trained to see and record the truth, to ignore the atrocities reassuring them that their sons were safe. "I, pure from the war, muff everything, get underpaid by radio, the *New Yorker* asks me for money back, *Collier's* wants some rewriting," she wrote to Hemingway. "Ho for the Causa." She had been right to dread the repercussions of her now public affair with Hemingway, for Pauline had decided to follow him to Spain, and by the time he reached Paris himself, she was waiting for him at the Hôtel Elysée. Their reunion was stormy. Hemingway was feeling ill, and had something wrong with his liver; he was also anxious about his articles for NANA, the North American Newspaper Alliance, and *To Have and Have Not* had just been released in the States, to poor reviews. Pauline threatened to jump off the hotel balcony. She told Hemingway that Martha was egoistic, selfish, stupid, childish, phony, and "almost without talent." They traveled home together on the *Grisholm,* and Hemingway admitted to Max Perkins that he was indeed in a "gigantic jam."

In January, Martha set off on a tour of lectures on Spain and the lessons of the war, and in her talks, praising the young Americans who had flocked to fight with the republicans, she returned to her old theme about the sense of dignity and morality "which only comes to people who know why they are there." On January 7, she was at the University of Minnesota, speaking to 3,000 people; three weeks later, she reached St. Louis, where the *Post-Dispatch* described her as an "honest partisan" and quoted her as calling Franco a "butcher." Everywhere she went, she was interviewed, and the articles that appeared in local papers were admiring. She brought to the platform, observed the reporter in Louisville, "the voice, the culture, the art of pose, the poise, gesture, diction which succeed upon the stage at its best," adding that this "slip of a girl" had been the best performer of the evening. The *New York Times* listed her name among those of the very few popular women lecturers of 1938. And everywhere she went, Martha warned of worse things to come if the Nationalists were allowed to defeat the democratically elected republican government of Spain. "Martha Gellhorn Predicts U.S. Will Soon Be in War," announced one headline. But the mood of America was not on her side, and even Eleanor Roosevelt, who had become an ever more passionate advocate for the republicans, was now under attack by the Catholic hierarchy, while Roosevelt refused to countenance any softening of the embargo.

In February, exhausted by delivering twenty-two lectures in less than a month, angry about America's isolationist foreign policy, sick of seeing herself as "Moses with the tablets of stone," and having lost twelve pounds, Martha pleaded ill health, canceled her last few lectures, and fled to Florida with her mother, to lie in the sun. But not for long. To Mrs. Roosevelt, who had written to urge her to "stop thinking for a little while," she replied that she had no mechanism to do so, and what was more, she felt she had no right to stop thinking. "The only way I can pay back for what fate and society have handed me is to try, in minor totally useless ways, to make an angry sound against injustice." On March 4, she met Hemingway in Miami. When news reached them that Franco had retaken Teruel and was driving a wedge through to the Mediterranean, splitting the Loyalist forces in two, they hurried back to Spain. Pauline did not go with them.

On board the *Queen Mary,* her handwriting uneven in her evident haste to write, Martha covered twelve pages in a letter to Mrs. Roosevelt. It was a furious cry about Spain and what she was now sure was a coming European war. "The young men will die," she wrote. "The best ones will die first, and the old powerful men will survive to mishandle the peace. . . . And all the people I love will finish up dead, before they can have done their work. . . . I wish I could see you. But you wouldn't like me much. I have gone angry to the bone."

The front line was the place to be now, where she did not have to think.

Long after the war in Spain was over, Martha wrote a short story called "Till Death Do Us Part." It was about a war photographer named Bara, an elusive Hungarian who wore flamboyant clothes and whose past was sealed off to everyone, together with all talk about his wife, Suzy, killed in a Nationalist raid in Spain. Bara was an attractive man, with glossy black hair, and he spent money, lots of money, with no regard for anything. He had a very good friend, a Pole named Lep, a "hit and run" photographer like himself, and an American girlfriend, Helen, a pleasant, reasonable woman, who was desperate to marry him. But, crucially, Bara had another friend, a woman he called Marushka, a war reporter he had met in Spain. Marushka and Bara were never lovers, but they had a friendship of great intimacy. They quarreled over everything, and they shouted at each other, but they minded a great deal whenever the other was in trouble. Of all the short stories she wrote, Martha liked this one the best. "I love it for what and who it is about," she told a friend, "knowing that it is truer than truth."

Martha met Robert Capa in Spain, soon after returning to the war in September 1938. Capa, a Hungarian by birth, the son of a dress-maker in Budapest, was by then Spain's most famous war photographer, his "moment of death" picture of a Loyalist soldier, caught as he is shot and begins to fall, having been picked up from *Vue* by *Life* and reprinted all around the world. As with Martha, what drew Capa was the effect of tragedy on ordinary people; like her, he was not all that keen on objectivity, saying that as a reporter "you must have a position or you cannot stand what goes on."

Capa was twenty-four, almost five years younger than Martha, and spoke poor English. Hemingway also liked Capa, who said he felt like his adopted son. Soon he had become one of the "trench buddies." But for Martha it was more than that; it was a friendship of a very particular sort. She often told people, "He was my brother, my real brother." Writing to Rosamond Lehmann in the early 1950s, she explained that she had had five friends in her life, all men, "when it is as if you were nearly the same," and of these Capa had been the "best, the nearest in every way." Neither for Capa nor for the others had she felt the slightest sexual attraction. Nevertheless: "They and the dead have always mattered to me more than any lovers. . . . Lovers somehow never seemed serious; there was something I couldn't quite believe—and even in the most anguishing intoxicating depths of a love affair, I would always rather be with my friends, who were my own people and where I belonged. . . . I only loved the world of men—not the world of men-and-women." Wars belonged to the world of men, and it was in wars that Martha found her closest friends.

Like Bara in the story, Capa had a wife, Gerda, killed by a reversing tank in Spain; he had a great photographer friend, David Seymour, whom he called Chem; and after the war, back in America, Ingrid Bergman fell very much in love with him and wanted to marry him, telling Martha that she had never before met "a free human being" like him. But Capa slipped away from her. In the sixteen years before Capa stepped on a mine south of Hanoi and was killed, he and Martha had a lot of fun. They talked about many things, Capa in his broken English, but they never talked about Gerda. They laughed all the time.

Barcelona, already a city reduced by war to extreme poverty and hunger, became, in March 1938, the scene of the most sustained aerial bombing of the Spanish war, providing an image of what was soon to follow throughout Europe. At ten-fifteen on the night of the sixteenth, under a full moon, Heinkel bombers began to pound the city. In the next forty-eight hours, they carried out eighteen raids, and many of the bombs fell on the city's most densely inhabited quarters, where tall buildings, housing dozens of families, lined narrow streets. Families were trapped under falling beams and bricks and mortar. At daybreak, reporters described scenes of carnage, and blood literally flowing down the gutters. Matthews later wrote in a dispatch that he had witnessed "things which Dante could not have imagined." Soon, Barcelona's hospitals were full of badly injured and dying survivors, and when Martha went to visit one ward she found "all the children silent in the white tiled room, white with huge black eyes." Barcelona had almost no food left, and everyone was hungry. It had long since run out of soap, and later Martha would remember the terrible smell, and the way that in the Hotel Majestic where they stayed, the linen, filthy and stained, would be ironed and put back on the beds.

The Loyalist troops were forced to retreat, and Martha and Hemingway followed the line of smashed and abandoned trucks, taking shelter behind low stone walls to watch the fascist bombers, "high and bright like dragon flies" glinting in the sun far above. When they came in to drop their loads, they made an echo that circled the mountains. One day Martha and Hemingway drove through the olive groves to the Mediterranean, where the water was as flat as glass, leaving a thin, lacy-white line of foam along the sand, and where the umbrella pines stood in clumps along the shoreline. The pink almond blossoms were out. They came on Modesto's headquarters and talked about the campaign with the general, who was wearing espadrilles and seemed dirty and tired, eating mutton chops and salad with sardines, and drinking wine from an empty can. Later, they drove back to Madrid and visited the hospital where Freddy Keller, the young American from the Abraham Lincoln Brigade, who had rescued eighteen of his men by twice swimming across the Ebro under fire, was recovering from a bullet wound in his thigh.

On April 15, Franco's troops reached the Mediterranean, splitting Barcelona from Valencia and Madrid. The rebel victories across Catalonia were emptying villages one after the other, and there were refugees everywhere, struggling along the roads, crouching in the ditches, taking shelter in bombed-out houses. "There were those who came with only a bundle," wrote Martha in her diary that day, Good Friday, 1938, "pink or yellow or blue or dirty grey, and all strange shapes, clutched under their arms or balanced on their heads, some walking fast and others wearily . . . leaving behind them everything to walk down mountain footpaths away from the enemy, in the dark. Their faces were the same, children's faces and the faces of the old men in twisted black stocking caps. Sad and tired and frightened but as if they had been frightened for a long time."

On April 18, the Italians captured Tortosa, and Martha and Hemingway, standing peeling hard-boiled eggs and eating oranges in an olive grove, watched as twenty-three bombers, small, delicate, and white against the sky, dropped their loads. Along the route there were pockets of Loyalist soldiers, some of the newer recruits still children, and men from the International Brigades, reading maps, smoking quietly, planning to make a last stand to give others the time to retreat. Borrowing her language from Hemingway, Martha wrote: "And maybe history is a stinking mess and a big injustice anyhow, and the victory is always wrong. But one thing is sure: good men are as absolute as mountains and as fine, and as long as there are any good men then it is worth while to live and be with them. And one cannot feel utterly hopeless about the future knowing that such people exist, whether they win or not. Though every day war seems more loathsome and the destruction of good people . . . more tragic and useless." There was no time, now, to be bored.

Martha wanted to stay on in Barcelona to write about the refugees and the evacuation of the wounded, and sent a cable to *Collier's* that it was all very like the "last days of Pompeii"; but world attention had moved away from the dying Spanish republic. "Not interested Barcelona story stop," *Collier's* replied. "Stale by the time we publish." The magazine wanted her to go to France, and then on to England and Czechoslovakia, to see what the rest of Europe felt about a war. *Collier's* offered excellent rates—$1,000 for each piece it accepted—and in any case she could hardly turn down the assignment. But she had come to love and care about Spain, and was still thinking of writing about it in the way she had written about the depression, and she still believed that what happened in Spain was "the affair of us all, who not sex? Soon, the exercises began to turn into stories, even if some of them remained little more than descriptions—of a drunken evening with the pelota players in Havana, of a walk in Madrid during the civil war—with an emotional charge to lend some bite. But two are revealing, both for their content and their edgy tone. "Portrait of a Lady" is a bitter tale about an attractive American reporter who seduces a heroic Finnish aviator, only to find herself discarded with disdain. The second of the longer stories is "Good Will to Men," in which the heroine—another American woman reporter—travels home to the States from an assignment in Finland, stopping in Paris, where she hopes to persuade influential friends to intervene on behalf of a sick, interned, former soldier with the International Brigades (quite unmistakably, a portrait of Gustav Regler, now confined in a French camp and ill). What stands out about both stories, apart from the fact that they are so largely autobiographical, is the nastiness of the characters and the unpleasant trace they leave in the mind. Six years of observing and writing about the suffering of powerless people had left Martha with profound misgivings about the selfishness of those with power.

Sometime during the spring of 1940, Hemingway bought a radio so that he and Martha would "get our disasters shrieked fresh and on the minute" without waiting for the newspaper to arrive by the mail boats. Martha, in particular, wanted to follow the war in Europe and tried to persuade an increasingly reluctant Hemingway to involve himself in world affairs, but Hemingway found the daily bulletins intrusive and finally banned the radio from the house altogether, saying that he wanted no news until his book was finished, and the war would still be there waiting for him. She found his detachment irritating, and though she greatly admired the bits of the book he had allowed her to look at, she complained that he was like an animal with his work, keeping it squirreled away in a drawer. Evidently, there had been difficulties between them, for Hemingway wrote her a long letter of apology for having been "thoughtless, egotistic, mean-spirited and unhelpful" over the past eighteen months, putting it down to pressures of the book, and telling her that he would absolutely understand if she decided that she didn't want to go ahead with their marriage. It was a generous letter from "your Bongie . . . who loves you and who understands whatever you want to do even if you don't want to marry him."

In June, Martha took off for New York, saw her friends and her publishers, and lunched with Allen Grover. She was there at the fall of France and talked gloomily about "those goddam maniac bastards" destroying the beauty of Paris. When she returned to Cuba, after a few nights in the White House, she took Edna with her, who liked Hemingway and got on well with him. They went out on the *Pilar* and one day saw a rare whale shark, as big as the boat. Martha reported happily to Hortense Flexner that as the days passed, her mother looked better and younger and happier than at any time since her father had died; she said that she now felt in an odd way as if she were the older of the two, and tougher in the sense that she was less startled by evil, and "not being a very good person myself I can take a lot of nongood." There was one outburst, when Hemingway failed to turn up for dinner and Martha stormed into the bar in Havana where he was sitting drinking and bawled him out for keeping Edna waiting, but Cuba had rarely seemed to her such an agreeable and tranquil place, nor her need to live a simple and private life more acute.

In September, Hemingway went alone to New York to prepare for the publication of *For Whom the Bell Tolls*. Scribner's had cleared its shop windows on Fifth Avenue and given the entire space over to a display of his work, and the first printing of 75,000 was already sold out by the time he arrived. Maria's blond hair, "like a wheatfield in the wind," was perceived to be very like Martha's own, but in all other ways Hemingway's modest and compliant heroine could not be mistaken for the assertive and independent Martha. There were offers from Hollywood for the film rights, and at some point there was even talk of Martha—to whom, together with Herbert Matthews, the book was dedicated—taking the part of Maria. The *New York Times Book Review,* in a front-page article, called it the "best, deepest, and truest book" that Hemingway had written. Only a small number of communist reviewers attacked the book, accusing Hemingway of exploiting the Loyalist cause. His old friend Alvah Bessie was one of three veterans of the Abraham Lincoln Brigade who signed an open letter denouncing him for "mutilating" the cause of democracy by slandering André Marty, maligning La Passionara, the communist orator and writer, and exaggerating the influence of the Soviet Union on the republicans. None of this had any negative effect on sales. As Hemingway wrote to Hadley, "book selling like frozen Daiquiris in hell." From Martha, still in Cuba, came loving letters, saying that she felt that the two of them were now like "peas in a pod," and that it felt lonely and very chilly without him.

In the autumn of 1940, taking the boys with them, Martha and Hemingway returned to Sun Valley. Hemingway, liberated from his book, organized daily expeditions along the creeks and up into the mountains. Locals referred to him fondly as the "General." Bumby fished "as if the whole fate of mankind depended on it," Gigi was a boy clearly "geared to get on," but twelve-year-old Mouse was the boy whose character most intrigued Martha. To Max Perkins, she wrote that he would certainly go somewhere, and that wherever that was, it would be "a place to envy . . . a fine ungrabby certain kind of place." She thought they were "rare" boys, borrowing a word that Hemingway had used all the time in his novel, and said that Hemingway had a huge talent for being a father, bringing them up with "genius and not obeying any of the rules." For their part, the boys seemed increasingly attached to her, finding that her naturalness with children made her an easy companion. Many years later, Bumby told a reporter that she was the first "attractive lady I ever heard use the 'f' word."

They were joined at Sun Valley by Dorothy Parker and her husband, with whom they played tennis, and by Gary Cooper, who had starred in the 1932 film version of *A Farewell to Arms*. There was talk that he might now take the part of Robert Jordan in the proposed film version of *For Whom the Bell Tolls*. There had also been rumors that Dorothy Parker might write the script, but Hemingway had never liked her writing; Ingrid Bergman was now being suggested for the role of Maria, and Martha wrote to Hortense Flexner that if Greta Garbo "were a braver actress . . . she might do Pilar, without eyelashes, but with all the strength there is in her, unused and never to be used." Martha continued to love the untouched country, and the local people, whom she considered to be "individuals without being Dali," but she found the "famous folk . . . a pain in the ass" and was appalled by their constant talk of box office returns. "I begin to feel my family is directly descended from Martin Luther," she wrote to Max Perkins, "as I get angrier and angrier about such idiocies." She was maliciously delighted when Cooper's wife, Rocky, told her how much she sympathized with the central character in Henry James's *Portrait of a Lady*. "Having a living bitch meet a fictional bitch and feel the sisterhood at once, is my idea of doing a good job." Martha decided to divide up the "movie element" around her into the "good" and the "intolerable" and one night lectured them all, after a prolonged bout of heavy drinking, on the evils of Hollywood for serious writers. Money was about to start pouring in for the film rights to *For Whom the Bell Tolls*, and she and Hemingway agreed that there was very little they actually wanted to spend it on, other than a new icebox for the Finca Vigia, some binoculars, and a sleeping bag. If she was jealous of Hemingway's huge success, she showed no sign of it.

For all her protestations about a peaceful life, however, Martha had no talent for being a happy vegetable. With France now partly in German hands, with the Italians entering the war, and with the British enduring nightly bombing raids, she longed to be in Europe. "How I wish I were a journalist again," she wrote to John Gunther, "that life of rushing and asking questions, trying to tell the liars from the ones who maybe know the facts. . . . Sun Valley is a kind of Shangri-La, without the Tibetan odors. (But where I want to be, boy, is where it is all blowing up.)" To Grover, she wrote that she so hated "not to be part of history (I don't want to be elected or anything or mentioned in the papers, I just want to be where history is happening, to see it, to know about it for myself, to do whatever small goofy usually futile thing I can do in order to make some minor events easier for unknown people)."

News of Hemingway's uncontested divorce from Pauline on grounds of desertion came through on November 4, and Robert Capa arrived soon after to take photographs of Hemingway and Martha for *Life*. They show Martha, her hair windswept, wearing a slightly rueful smile, in various sporting settings, often in shorts, her long legs stretched out, and they caught a look somewhere between happiness and self-mockery. Martha told Hortense Flexner that being engaged gave her a feeling of permanent youth, and her new diamond-and-sapphire ring was "snappy as hell." Perhaps reflecting on the unpleasantness of Hemingway's divorce from Pauline, she seemed rather unsure about the marriage itself, writing to Grover, "I would rather sin respectably, any day of the week. . . . Allen, it's awful, isn't it, the way you can make someone pay you in stocks and bonds and furniture and Christ knows what all, for not loving you. I thought if people stopped loving you, you went into a corner like a sick animal and held yourself very tight, so as not to break. . . . I like it better clean: I think sin is very clean. . . . There is all the deadly obligation of one human being to another, but there is no insurance. You are probably less free, socially, but anyhow you feel awful simple and straight in your heart." Her misgivings upset Hemingway, who wrote her a brief note one day about her ratting on their plans and giving him a "good sound busted heart." The moment passed. Edna, also clearly very anxious about the marriage, tried hard to persuade them to wait until they were quite certain; but by now the train was moving.

On November 21, in the dining room of the Union Pacific Railroad at Cheyenne, Wyoming, Martha and Hemingway were married. Martha was thirty-two, Hemingway forty. There was an affectionate telegram from the Roosevelts, and several newspapers carried the story, listing Martha's achievements as a writer and adding that she had been married once before, to Bertrand de Jouvenel. One reporter called it a "pairing of flint and steel." "Ernest and I belong tightly to each other," Martha told Mrs. Roosevelt. "We are a good pair and we are both crazy about being married." F. Scott Fitzgerald, on hearing of the event, remarked that it was very odd to think of Hemingway married to a "really attractive woman": "I think the pattern will be somewhat different than with his Pygmalion-like creations." After the short ceremony, they ate roast moose for dinner.

Many years later, when Martha was approaching seventy, she wrote a book about the horror journeys of her life, *Travels with Myself and Another*. It is the funniest of her books, full of comic stories of punishing discomfort, embarrassing situations, paralyzing boredom, excruciating delays, and bitter and heartfelt clashes between travelers condemned to share ghastly experiences in some foreign and distant land. Perhaps the most comic expedition of all is an account of a trip to the Far East with Hemingway, very soon after they got married, which he insisted on referring to as their honeymoon. In the book, Hemingway is "UC," Unwilling Companion. The three months she spent in the Far East, Martha later said, taught her a new lesson about war, and about what utter hell it was for all the people who were not fighting. What is most memorable about "Mr. Ma's Tigers," her chapter on the Far East, is its affectionate, appreciative, and self-mocking tone. Given that biographers have tended to paint Martha's relationship with Hemingway as only quarrelsome and exploitative, it is an agreeable and wholly convincing account of shared laughter.

place waiting to be filled. Do not believe much in loneliness (same way you do not believe in suffering). . . . really believe it is man's fate, in whatever doses it comes." Hemingway tried to steady her nerve, again telling her that writers who indulged themselves in too much wallowing in self-doubt were contemptible. Martha seldom allowed herself to sound vulnerable, especially with Hemingway. But now, nearing the end of her book, she had a moment of frailty. "I wish we could stop it all now," she wrote to him, "the prestige, the possessions, the position, the knowledge, the victory. And by a miracle, return together under the arch at Milan, you so brash in your motorcycle sidecar and I badly dressed, fierce, loving. . . . That loud reckless dishevelled girl was a better person. . . . You have been married so much and so long that I do not believe it can touch you where you live and that is your strength. It would be terrible if it did because you are so much more important than the women you happen to be married to." Their letters to each other, at this point, were still fond. On June 23, Hemingway wrote to describe the camp he and his two younger sons had set up on an island, where they had caught and penned two giant turtles and were fattening up a pig, which went swimming in the sea. He was still very uneasy about his position over the war in Europe. "You have a fine time at wars and love them maybe or happiest at them. . . . But by God I hate them."

On June 27 Martha put down the last words of her novel. Writing to tell Perkins that it was finally done, she said that it had come out at 90,000 words. When he asked her for a couple of sentences for a blurb, she replied, "It's about love and loneliness, I think, but who can say?" It was also about the rottenness of governments. In a refrain that was now making its way into all her writing, Martha has the young French teacher Pierre say, "People are good and governments are bad." To H. G. Wells, Martha wrote that she was sorry for her heroine, betrayed by both the men in her novel: "But on the whole I am sorry for women. They are not free: there is no way they make themselves free." Freedom, solitude, responsibility—the dicta she grew up with, shaped by the twists in her own life.

There were now struggles to find a good title, and *Share of Night, Share of Morning,* from a poem by Emily Dickinson, was settled on, though Hemingway urged her to consult Ecclesiastes and Proverbs, saying that while the New Testament had been exhaustively mined, the

Old Testament still contained much that might be useful. There was a moment of anxiety, when readers at Scribner's worried that sales might be affected because the heroine was a mulatto, and Hemingway objected that the book was seriously short of commas and reduced the galleys to a red battlefield with squiggles on every page; and then the novel was done. Martha dedicated it to her mother.

Hemingway had not spent much time at the Finca that spring, but when he was there he drank heavily with his *Pilar* submarine hunters or went off to spend long evenings in the Floridita. By now he had quarreled with most of his writer friends and preferred to spend his time with fellow sportsmen. Their life together was beginning to show signs of strain, with Martha no longer as ready as she had once been to overlook Hemingway's boundless egotism. She was now openly scornful of his spying activities and accused him of becoming boastful and self-aggrandizing; she hated the stories he spun and weaved over the whiskey during the drunken evenings. She was finding his sloppiness and the dirtiness of his clothes almost impossible to bear. He, in turn, told her that her cleanliness was obsessive. He complained to friends that she did not understand about money, saving "terrifically" on pennies and spending larger sums without a thought. The laughter and jokes were not as much fun any longer. One night, after a row about his erratic drunken driving, she insisted on taking the wheel of his much loved Lincoln Continental. He slapped her, and Martha drove it slowly but deliberately straight into a tree, got out, and walked home, leaving him with the wreck.

Making love with Hemingway had never been much pleasure for Martha, who still found sexual relations less a matter of happiness than an awkward obligation. She told a friend many years later that she had been astonished to discover, talking to Tillie Arnold during one of her visits to Sun Valley, that making love was actually something women could enjoy. From remarks made at various times by both of them, it seems probable that Martha had an abortion at about this time. The moment for them to have the daughter Hemingway had wanted had clearly passed, though whether it had ever really existed for Martha is impossible to say. Restless, feeling herself isolated from events in Europe she longed to be part of, and now frequently quarreling with Hemingway, the idea of children was not appealing. "You write about them so well and so poignantly," he told her, "and don't give a goddam about them."

The good times were not quite over; but they were growing fewer. Even so, Hemingway was angry when Martha told him that she had decided to go to Europe for *Collier's* to report on the war, even without formal military accreditation. She pressed him to go with her, but he balked at the idea of leaving Cuba and the submarine hunting. With some annoyance, accusing her of picking quarrels in order to justify her longing to get away, and telling her that she had turned into a prima donna as a writer, he made plans to spend three months on a wider sweep of the sea during her absence.

Just the same, they parted on an amicable, even tender note. "I will think of you so carefully all the time that you will be protected," Martha wrote as she left for New York, where she was to meet Colebaugh and Max Perkins and see the page proofs of her novel. She begged him to be careful of the bright sun reflecting off the sea, saying that she was happy to be his daughter but did not wish to see him become Milton. "You belong to me," she wrote. "Some time the war will be over. . . . We have a good wide life ahead of us. And I will try to be beautiful when I am old, and if I can't do that I will try to be good. I love you very much." Hemingway's reply was equally fond. "Live alone makes jumpy," he wrote back, "we will unjumpy ourselves . . . in the six foot bed and all the long hours talking by the pool." They had agreed on a code for Martha's letters from Europe, so that she could tell him where she was going without falling foul of the censor: a visit to Capa would stand for Africa, while Herbert Matthews would mean Italy. Sometime before she left, Hemingway wrote a letter in which he reminded her of Rilke's lines: "Love consists in this: that two solitudes protect and touch and greet each other." Then he went on: "I haven't protected you good and touched you little and have been greeting you scoffingly. But truly I respect and admire you very much and of this date and hour have stopped scoffing; which is the worst of all I think." Hemingway's own plan to leave Havana had fallen through, and he was going to be staying on alone at the Finca, sleeping on the floor with the cats, as he told Charles Scribner, who hunted for mice in his beard. He had now written nothing for over a year and was beginning to doubt that he would write anything again until after the war.

By September 3, having checked the proofs for her novel, its title now changed to *Liana*, Martha was installed in the Berkshire, a smart hotel on New York's East Side, where she embarked on a concentrated regime of exercises, face treatments, vitamin injections, and dentist and hair appointments, having decided that her gums were receding, that her hair was too dry, and that she would have to get her handmade shoes rebuilt to withstand the rigors of the war correspondent's life. After many consultations by mail with Hemingway, and appointments with different hairdressers, she had her hair cut very short, permed around the sides, and colored a "tawny brownish gold." When not out buying fashionable hats (shaped, she complained, as if for gnomes) and gray suits, or having the skin under her eyes peeled and her neck and chin tightened with expensive creams and treatments, she lunched and dined with friends. But she was soon complaining to Hemingway that the months in Cuba had left her ill at ease with New York society life, she felt bored and boring, and that nothing was fun in the way she had hoped it would be. As often when bored and gloomy, she felt ill and fretted about her weight and the fact that her face looked "jowly." New York, she reported, was full of horribly thin and unescorted women, and she found the whole thing scary, which made her reflect on how much she missed Hemingway, "really sick-eningly; I'm like somebody who crossed the river Styx by mistake and got in with a lot of spooks and left its real comrade elsewhere." One evening she had drinks with Dorothy Parker—who put away eight martinis in a couple of hours—and was once again both captivated by her "evil fascination" and repelled by her "worthless, self-pitying and unwashed" presence. When fifteen-year-old Mousie was able to take a day off from boarding school, he came to New York, and as always with Hemingway's sons, Martha was fond and appreciative.

By the end of the third week in September, when her passage for Europe had still not come through, she moved to a small suite at the Gladstone Hotel, which at $175 a month was cheaper than her room at the Berkshire, and which she filled with plants to make it look more like home. As Bumby would later observe, Martha was always excel-lent at making nests, being someone who felt insecure if her immediate surroundings did not please her, even if she was not always so good at running them. A friend sent her maid to do Martha's mending and washing. As the days passed, she added new bits of furniture—lamps, trays, glasses—and pinned photographs of Hemingway, the Finca, and the cats up on the walls, writing to tell him that she felt joined to him as to a Siamese twin and that she could imagine no future that did not include him. Apart, and feeling a little guilty, she quickly forgot the fights.

When not shopping or having beauty treatments, Martha was seeing her novel through the last stages before publication. She was irritated when a prepublication notice referred to her only as the "wife of Ernest Hemingway," but the signs for the book were all promising: a Swedish publisher had asked to buy the rights, the Theater Guild had expressed an interest, Paramount was talking about a film, and the Book-of-the-Month Club was considering it. With her much loved brother Alfred teaching medical students for the war effort and very short of money, she was planning to give him the $15,000 it would bring in if selected by the book club. She was miserable when she learned that it had been passed over. She appeared to mind less, however, when the renowned Miss Helburn of the Theater Guild interviewed her in a lordly manner and informed her that since her story of love and betrayal between a mulatto girl and two white men smacked too strongly of miscegenation, the part of Liana would probably have to be rewritten as a white girl if the guild were to take it. "There is no more brains or talent or courage in the theater than in the movies," she noted crossly. "It's all shit. The way I feel is: all passes, books alone remain. A book is a hard beautiful unperishable thing." After Max Perkins chose a photograph of her sitting on a rock laughing, her hair flying in the wind, she said it made her look like an aging Colette. She was just as sharp with a possible new agent, telling him that all decisions, however small, about her work were to be left to her, and that he was not to interfere.

The days of waiting turned into weeks, but by now she was back in the swim of New York, frenetically keeping up with parties and old friends passing through on their way to the war in Europe, and spending weekends in Washington with the Roosevelts, who introduced her to ambassadors and other useful contacts for London. Her old boss Harry Hopkins, who had been very ill, was now more or less permanently resident in the White House, as was Lorena Hickok, and Eleanor Roosevelt, as driven and active as ever, continued to cook scrambled eggs herself on Sunday nights for a passing assortment of friends. Martha's meetings with Colebaugh had gone well, and he had asked her to do one long piece on England, and then any number of shorter ones of 1,000 words or less: "the easiest thing for me to write . . . specific stories of specific people: what they wear, eat, say, how they are "way everyone has now become a great FFI or partisan and the way no one has served the Germans. . . . People are saying to each other in Paris 'What did you do during the war?' " With her distaste for cliques, she kept away from the smart hotels, like the Prince de Galles, where soldiers she dismissed as "very braided," the nonfighting generals and the quartermasters, went to drink, all of them "punks and grafters."

She also kept carefully away from Hemingway, though it was hard to ignore his hostility. He was not a man accustomed to being left by women, and his furious accounts to friends of their crumbling marriage made it plain that he was determined to emerge as the one who had had enough. "I hate to lose anyone who can look so lovely and who we taught to shoot and write so well," he wrote to his son Patrick, at boarding school in the States. "But have torn up my tickets on her." Though not always very pleasant to Mary—one day he told her she looked like a spider—he addressed her affectionately as "Small Friend" and, when not drinking with his entourage, took her on drives to see the Paris he had loved in the 1920s. There was no talk of drinking Tavel and reading *Le Sport* with Martha in a café.

The Allies, who had commandeered 700 hotels for their own use, had designated the Hotel Scribe as press headquarters, and it was here that gas was stored, along with coffee, champagne, and K rations, and that reporters brought their stories to be read by the censors. Martha, though still a pariah in the eyes of the military, managed to slip in some cables for *Collier's*. Harold Acton, to whom fell the task of censoring them, later said that her stories were among the most acute that he passed. After the Allies revealed that they had discovered Gestapo torture chambers on the grounds of the Ministry of Aviation, in the Avenue Foche, and at Chaton in the suburbs, Martha joined a tour arranged by the press office and later wrote about what she called the "wounds" of Paris. Very simply, she described seeing dark wet tunnels, much of the ground under water, where captives were held until they died; a cemetery, where men and women wandered, searching for lost relations, taken away during the war by the Germans; and a shack still brown with dried blood, where a prisoner had scratched on the wall, "Revenge me." In the years of their occupation, the Germans were said to have shot 30,000 people and tortured many others, some to death. Now the *"épuration"* of those who had helped them was under way, the head shaving and summary trials and executions.

The formal trials of writers and journalists who were considered to have collaborated were about to begin. On September 9, two weeks after the liberation, a manifesto of French writers, signed by fifty-nine leading intellectuals, among them Paul Valéry and François Mauriac, called for the "just punishment of usurpers and traitors," and by October it had 156 names on its blacklist. The trials of writers proceeded quickly, if only because it was a simple matter to read what they had written.

Bit by bit, Martha learned what had happened to those friends of hers and Bertrand's who had been so much in favor of an alliance with Germany before the war. Some, she discovered, had disappeared abroad, like Bertrand himself, who, having served as a private on the Maginot Line, had gone to Switzerland in 1942 after realizing that he could not actually prove that he had remained friends with Otto Abetz solely in order to provide information to the Free French. (Abetz had been appointed German ambassador to Paris in 1940.) Among these former friends, now abroad or lying low, were the "passive" collaborators, writers like André Gide or Henry de Montherlant, who had seen in the French defeat something more profoundly wrong with France than military unpreparedness, and had simply tried to make the best of the occupation. Others, like Sacha Guitry, Jean Luchaire, and Robert Brasillach, editor of the pro-Nazi *Je Suis Partout*, were already in prison and would soon be executed.

Abetz himself was under arrest and would receive a twenty-year prison sentence from a Paris military tribunal. Responsible for the "Otto List" of some 1,200 banned French and foreign books—including most English translations and all books written by Jews—Abetz would also be held accountable for the deportation of Jews from Drancy. Bertrand's offer to appear as a witness at his trial was refused. Not long after his release, Abetz died in a mysterious car crash on the Cologne-Ruhr autobahn, when the steering on his car failed; it was said to have been tampered with as a revenge for the deportations.

Another of Martha's friends, Pierre Drieu la Rochelle, had tried to kill himself two weeks before the liberation. He would try again while in the hospital, by cutting his wrists, and was again saved. He would succeed eight months later, on his third attempt. Having returned to Paris, where he was ostracized by his friends and summoned to appear before a tribunal, he swallowed three tubes of sleeping pills and turned on the gas. "He failed with his death," wrote a reporter for the resistance *Franc-Tireur,* "as he failed with life." In the winter of 1944, after his second attempt at suicide, Drieu had kept a secret diary. "I do not want to be an intellectual who prudently measures his words," he had written. "We must dirty our feet, at least, but not our hands. . . . I am no ordinary patriot, no limited nationalist: I am an internationalist. I am not only a Frenchman, I am a European."

Even Colette, whose husband, Maurice Gondeket, was Jewish, had a slight cloud hanging over her, because she had written for the collaborationist paper *Le Petit Parisien.* And both Arletty, the singer, and Coco Chanel, who had taken German lovers and lived at the Ritz, were briefly arrested. Arletty had had her hair shaved.

In "A Honeyed Peace," a short story written after the war about Paris soon after liberation, Martha is less absolute and censorious than in much of her earlier fiction. The story revolves around two foreign women, one English and one American, who return to Paris with the Allies and discover that their close French friend Evangeline has been ostracized by smart society as well as by local tradesmen because her husband, Renaud, has been arrested for collaboration. As the two women explore their own reactions and those of their former friends, there is both compassion and cynicism about the reckoning and the settled scores.

On September 4, the Allies took Brussels, and Martha traveled in their wake, once again eager to escape Hemingway and the drinking parties. She found the city in a frenzy of celebration and the Belgians more apparently delighted at their liberation than the Parisians, perhaps helped by the discovery of 80,000 looted bottles of the finest claret in the city's cellars. When, three days later, Antwerp was taken, the cages at the lion house at the zoo were emptied to make room for Germans and collaborators: one cage for German officers, a second for privates, a third for Belgian collaborators, and a fourth for their wives and daughters, and women who had slept with Germans. The captives sat on the straw, staring through the bars.

By the middle of September, Martha was on the move again, following behind the British ground forces trying to link up with the airborne divisions dropped at Arnhem, driving across the flat land through villages that looked, under the gray sky, like the industrial north of England. Nijmegen, a small Dutch town obliterated by shell-

When not at work on her regimental article, Martha had been spending her days with the other foreign correspondents, loafing about the city, an activity she had enjoyed since her first days as a young reporter in the press gallery of the League of Nations in Geneva. In particular she went around Berlin with CBS correspondent Charles Collingwood, who made her laugh. Gavin, she would say later, did not make her laugh. Soon, Dietrich informed Gavin that Martha was really in love with Collingwood, and a furious Gavin, telling Martha he was going out for a short walk, went to call on Dietrich and stayed away all night. Jealousy was not an emotion Martha had experienced before. But, recognizing the "disgusting, cheap, ugly" sensation that now overcame her, she left Berlin for Paris, declaring that no relationship with a man was ever going to work for her and that henceforth she would stick to friendship. To a weasely letter, in which Gavin tried to spread the blame for his misadventure on mutual friends, gossip, and the times, Martha responded with a ferocious blast. She was also clearly hurt, and astonished to find herself so. Marlene Dietrich, she said, was a cobra. As for herself, she had been foolish enough to love, trust, and admire him, and she described her reaction when she realized that he had gone to bed with Dietrich: "I stayed in that room weeping as I really did not believe I ever could or would again . . . and every night since it has come back to me the same way, like a pain that hurts too much." She was, she declared, through with him. Her plan was now to return to England to build herself "a sound adult life." "I have decided that men really want tarts and tarts is what they are going to get. . . . You can sleep with everyone you like including sing-song girls and goats. . . . After all, none of this matters much, does it. We are only two people, not desperately important people, and we always have a lot of work. Luckily."

Gavin began by sending first one aide, and then another, to Paris, and when these efforts failed to move her, he went there himself. They went to bed. It was, wrote Martha later, "more exciting physically" than it had ever been, but in part of her mind and heart she had already begun to draw away from him. In any case, they had very little time together in which to absorb what had become of their relationship, because Gavin was coming to the end of his posting in Berlin and Martha had arranged to write an article for the *New Yorker* about the Japanese surrender in Bali.

Early in March 1946, she set off for the Far East, later describing the surrender as an event of glorious confusion, in which Americans behaved with a spectacular lack of dignity and efficiency, and the surrendering Japanese, neat, elegant, and impassive in their pristine uniforms, handed over their swords rather as if they were giving away fountain pens. When the American troops saw that the Balinese girls had bare breasts, they broke into loud cheers; all breasts throughout Bali were at once covered.

To Robert Sherrod, correspondent for *Time* and *Life,* who had helped Martha with introductions in the Far East, she reported from Singapore that she felt she now needed to be alone for a bit, that she was "all shredded up inside" from the war and her parting from Hemingway, and that she had invented a new phrase she rather liked: "the pale empty color of the future." She did not take to Indonesia, referring to it as "that stinkhole," warning that the nationalism she saw everywhere was a fever chart by which to measure the sickness of the postwar world, and complaining that the Indonesians were niggardly, mean, and lacked stature. Something of the old bounce in her letters to close men friends had come back, a particular combination of intimacy, carefully circumscribed by self-deprecating humor, and distance, the repeated reassertion of independence, that occasionally made her sound flippant. She told Sherrod that she never intended to write another word about the Orient or indeed ever go there again. "It is hopeless and shitty; give the country back to the ants, I say." That night, she dreamed that she was in a Japanese prison camp and that she killed a smiling woman guard who had plunged her teeth into her arm.

What she really wanted, she wrote to Sherrod, using the throwaway asides that characterized the letters of her younger years, in which the things she cared about were packaged as jokes, was a little white house, with a picket fence around it and some toddlers; but she had probably already blown that and was condemned to eke out the remaining years in the company of the "semi-important middle-aged." To add to her sense of being alone, she received several long letters from Bill Walton, who had been in New York when Gavin led his 82nd Airborne Division, "natty and drilled like the Rockettes," in a great parade up Fifth Avenue, on a brilliant January morning, to cheers from the crowds lining the streets. The day had been declared a holiday by the city for the event.

Walton described a dinner given for the officers by the mayor, and the many parties attended by Charles Collingwood, Irwin Shaw, Allen Grover, and Capa that had followed, at which much drink had been consumed by all. "Capa has a thing with Ingrid Bergman," Walton wrote. "I think she really broke his soft Hungarian heart." Dietrich, whom he referred to as "the movie queen," had not been sighted. Walton himself was now pursuing Martha, though he kept his tone extravagantly self-mocking. "My little duck," he wrote, "the real trouble with me is that being with you has spoiled me completely for other women." He told her that a limerick about one of her introductions in the Far East, to the lieutenant governor-general of the Dutch East Indies, was now doing the rounds of their New York friends:

> Bulletin from Belgravia
> Marty's gone to Batavia
> With a guy named van Mook
> Who can't even Fook,
> Which is most unusual behavia!

Martha, caught up emotionally with Gavin, brooding about the collapse of Germany and the concentration camps, had thought little more about her play, though it had been written, as she told Grover, in her "life's blood." She and Virginia had given it to a young actress named Penelope Dudley Ward to read and been delighted when they heard her laugh out loud. Since then Virginia had efficiently found both an agent and a director, fresh from directing *Charlie's Aunt* in the prisoner-of-war camp in which he had spent the war. In June 1946 *Love Goes to Press*—a title they both hated—opened at the Embassy Theatre in Hampstead. Virginia's part, that of the reporter Jane, who coolly beat her male colleagues to a scoop, was played by a young woman who had been touring the troops, while a then-unknown Californian actress named Irene Worth became Annabelle, the Martha part. All the cast except for Worth were able to save on costumes by wearing their own war uniforms. It was a nice group of actors, Martha wrote to a friend, "with no fairies in it, which is a rest in London."

The first-night audience were appreciative of the antics of the two irreverent women who tied their male colleagues in knots of vanity and pomposity, and Annabelle's sardonic one-liners and self-deprecating asides made them laugh as much as did Martha's own with her friends. Words and expressions very familiar to those who knew Martha well—

"happy as a goat," "oh my," "chums"—filled dialogue that was neither very profound nor very subtle but was nonetheless still funny. The
critics were full of praise. Martha and Virginia, though delighted by
the laughter and the cheers, fled the theater when called to the stage
to speak at the end of the performance.

Martha was now fixing up her house off Eaton Square, describing
what she called her "little sewer" as "quite lovely," elegant and white
inside, though she told Robert Sherrod that the outside still looked like
"a camera study of blasted Europe." It was her eleventh home, and
after months of combing London for unobtainable luxuries like paint,
she was determined that it would be the last place she would ever
redecorate. By some strange alchemy, she wrote to Sherrod, she felt
unhurried and at peace in "this rain sodden burg" and was hopeful
that at last she was in sight of that "shining and always diminishing
goal: roots, a place of your own, peace." Like Virginia, she was convinced that she was unsuited for American life, telling Sherrod that
neither of them could imagine getting ahead if they went back to the
States, "being unable to see where the getting got you," a somewhat
disingenuous remark from one of the most successful—and hardly
retiring—woman journalists of the day. To compensate for the short-
ages and drabness of everything, and for the gray skies, she went out
a great deal, to restaurants and to parties and dancing, with friends
made through Virginia, fighting off a growing feeling that her working
life was going nowhere and that Gavin, who came to London to see
her, was not the man for her to marry. Already, she was finding him
less and less fun. Her women friends, on the other hand, she did find
fun, somewhat to her own surprise, "all so worldly and so funny, dis-
abused, unexcited, uncomplaining and a pleasure to look at." Martha
had never felt very close to women before, so much preferring her men
friends that it was no longer entirely as a joke that she talked of herself
as being one of the boys, and more like a man than a woman. She had
always been wary of the intimacy of women, their affection, the pat-
terns of conciliation and tentativeness.

When she was invited to the fiftieth anniversary dinner of the *Daily
Mail,* she wore the backless Schiaparelli evening dress she had worn at
the World Economic Conference thirteen years before. She wrote to a
friend: "My spine was the most visible thing in the room. I got waved
at, drunk to, and talked about by Mr Churchill (who said, 'Ah, so it's

lis, vastly outnumbered as people, had nonetheless as many soldiers and were better trained and better led. There were truces, brokered by the United Nations and Count Folke Bernadotte, the United Nations mediator in Palestine until he was assassinated by Israeli extremists. Early in 1949, an armistice of sorts was drawn up, leaving half the original Palestinians deprived of their lands, refugees who scattered into Lebanon, Syria, Transjordan, Egypt, and Kuwait. Some 4,000 Israelis had died, and while no reliable figure has ever been established, the Arab dead numbered at least four times as many.

For Martha, watching these events unfold, there had been nothing but a sense of relief and admiration. Israel was a country founded on the bones of six million dead Jews, murdered because there had been no place for them to go. It was as a human being, more than as a Jew, which even now played a remarkably small part in her thinking, that she felt so strongly.

"Tel Aviv, river of sand." she wrote in her notebook, as the plane came in to land on this first visit. "Powder puff clouds then a long patch of spotless sea and sky. . . . Excited and happy again. A new world." Capa was waiting for her at the Hotel Armon, which was small and shabby and close to the seafront, and he had already discovered a bar with good whiskey and martinis. They drank and talked about being Jews, the "feeling of Jewishness." Capa introduced her to Moshe Pearlman, a journalist who had been at London University and had come to Israel the moment the new state was declared, to run the press department for the foreign office and the army. He was funny and energetic, with a Groucho Marx mustache.

The three of them wandered around the streets of Tel Aviv, Martha stopping to question the people they met. One evening, as they were drinking in a rather scruffy bar after a day in the Negev Desert, discussing the fact that a soldier and his girl had been killed along the same stretch of road only hours after they had driven along it, an elegant figure in white tie and tails appeared. It was Leonard Bernstein, whose sister Capa knew in New York. Another day, Pearlman introduced them to "a young, curt, blond captain," slender and with an eye patch, named Moshe Dayan. To Martha and Capa, it seemed like old times in Spain. They belonged, not so much because they were Jews, but because they so profoundly shared Israel's hopes; it was a country, wrote Martha, that was not separated from her, and so instinctively familiar that she did not have to keep wondering about it. "We were all merry and elated. Something good had come out of the endless horror of the second world war, a new country full of young, brave, gay people and of hope. The courage was breathtaking." They went to Jaffa, to Haifa to see children learning Hebrew, to a kibbutz, to a Druze village, to a settlement of immigrants. One night they attended a Hanukkah party. "Very gay," wrote Martha in one of the two closely written notebooks that she kept of the trip, adding: "I still don't really do well at a dance." What struck her repeatedly was that everyone seemed happy, "sometimes like music in a hymn, sometimes like music to dance to," which was what made Israel different from other places. Italy was about its churches, Greece its ruins; but Israel was about surviving, and about feeling glad.

One night, Capa said to her that she should leave Mexico, that time was running out, and she should be in closer contact with the world. "But I don't want to," she wrote that night. "Why does everyone tell me this: is there some doubt or unhappiness about me, of which I'm not aware?" But she was restless, and her fatal tendency to grow impatient when too long in the company of others was returning. Three days later, she continued: "It is too ghastly to admit, I feel bored and frustrated. Something must be old and finished inside me, burned out. Because I am no longer open as once I was." The notes that followed were full of references to feeling "dreary," "heavy," "pretentious," and "self-centered." Israel, the new world, with its energy and sense of adventure and hope, was immensely seductive; but Martha's tastes and interests, if not her sympathies, lay with the old.

Martha wrote many letters about Israel, about the courage and the gaiety of the Jews, and about the stories of their lives, "a gold mine the equal of which I've never before seen." "I am now certain," she told Walton, "that gloominess and cowardice go together." She had laughed as she had not laughed in years with Capa and Pearlman and Bernstein, but she had not fallen in love, and all good journeys, she declared, ought to include falling in love; perhaps those days were over. Indeed, she said to Walton, her role these days was not so much that of sex queen as Queen Ant. Once back in Mexico, she was frantically busy.

With a small child and a nanny to look after, and Edna a frequent visitor, Martha had moved into a larger rented house on the Avenida del Parque, a cream-colored bungalow she described as the nastiest of the eight houses she had lived in since 1930. But its walled garden and flowering vines enchanted her, and she painted it white and filled it with plain furniture, obsessively consumed by a need to get every detail perfect before she felt right in it.

Martha remained overwhelmed by the love she felt for Sandy, and sent cards to friends with his photograph, on which she repeated his humorous sayings, and her own efforts to make him bold, by getting him to stand up to an imperious two-and-a-half-year-old neighbor. He had all the advantages of not having inherited her genes, she said: a sanguine nature, irresistible laughter, and huge enthusiasm. And he seemed to love and need her, which made her feel cheerful. She bought him clothes in the market, red and blue dungarees, which ran when they got wet, so that his skin was colored like a rainbow and he wove about on his short stout legs like a drunken gangster. She felt insanely proud of him, of his fat little body and his new words and the way he looked and smiled. She had not expected such happiness. Only Edna's steady presence and a flow of reassuring letters from Mrs. Roosevelt prevented total frenzy every time he sneezed or had a diaper rash. Her worry now was whether she could afford it all, and how she would raise the $7,000 needed to get proper residence papers for herself and Sandy. "A child is clearly twice as expensive as a yacht and a built-in mistress," she wrote to Walton.

The frivolous short stories were going well. After a ferociously boring local luncheon party, she resolved to stop writing about good innocent people, "the ones whom life does in because they are victims," and write instead "in high shrill hysterical notes about the people who are all right, and should be slaughtered. The ones who make life into a vast grey blur . . . the sprightly living dead, the utterly idle." The "vast grey blur" of life had a particular terror for Martha, and it was growing stronger.

She had turned against journalism and its intrusiveness, and her mind was filled with short stories, though Hemingway and his many cats refused to take shape, and she had rented a room nearby in which she wrote furiously. When, a few weeks later, first the *New Yorker* and then the *Atlantic* turned down her "*good* stories," she was mortified. "I don't want to be a bad writer, struggling in splendid isolation (and in vain) to do good work," she wrote miserably to Walton, to whom, together with Meyer, she sent almost weekly letters. "I'd rather know, and be a lousy writer, rolling in dough and idleness; I'd rather be something complete, not a grisly effort towards something not intended. Oh dear, do understand that sentence."

Soon after Christmas 1949, and with great reluctance, for she found the idea and the process of writing personal pieces a form of torture, she agreed to do an article about finding Sandy for the *Saturday Evening Post*. Linking a writer and his work was not only false, she insisted all her life, but limiting, and she was embarrassed in case friends found the story mawkish. But the editors at the *Post* were delighted and sent her a check for $2,250. "Little Boy Found" is a charming piece, very plain, and the *Post* published it in April 1950 together with a large photograph of Martha, looking down with a smile of quizzical pride at a very small, beaming Sandy, who is sitting on some steps in the sunshine.

After Edna left to go back to St. Louis, where she came down with hepatitis, Martha resumed her more solitary life, built now around Sandy's meals and bedtime. While he slept, she read, books found in Cuernavaca or sent from New York by Meyer, and it was with him that she kept up a literary correspondence, praising Rebecca West, her current heroine, for saying she was in favor of pleasure, enjoying the *Goncourt Journal* because it reassured her that life was just as lousy in the nineteenth century, and brooding over Arthur Mizener's life of F. Scott Fitzgerald, which reminded her all over again about how badly his friends had behaved toward him and how ashamed she felt of Hemingway's part in it.

She had begun to keep notes on Cuernavaca's foreign community, filing them alphabetically on index cards, and these would later make their way into a Mexican novel. More clearly than with any other book, perhaps, they show the extent of Martha's reliance on real characters for her fiction, the very sharpness of her reporter's eye lending a depth her imagination did not always provide. There was one woman, who gossiped disapprovingly about her neighbors, and Ernesto, a "lamentably indiscreet but v. kind doctor," who was accused of poisoning someone's wife. The tone of many of the entries is neutral; but Martha's eye could also be harsh. Ross and Vera "finally married when Vera five months gone. She very ugly . . . he drunk, pretentious, lives off her. Incredibly beastly." The unfortunate Vera's card has several entries. "Vera: vital, common: the way she dresses, exposing those vast bosoms. . . . The party for Allan's mother (in purple velvet) all fairies. And dismal." Allan was another fairy, with the look of a fox. There is something chilling in the neatness of the index cards and in the thought of Martha returning to fill them in with fresh observations after dinner parties.

Surrounded by these foxes and dismal fairies, Martha preferred to stay at home with Sandy, whose first sentences in English she delightedly relayed to friends in long letters about the pleasure of motherhood. People were put on Earth for only four reasons, she observed to Walton; to laugh with, and this she put first; to give a jet propulsion to the mind, because their minds were richer, faster, stranger, and deeper; to love, and this, interestingly, she placed third; and to go to bed with. Children did not rate a mention. Since Cuernavaca provided her with none of these, she kept her company for Sandy, except when visitors came through from abroad, though Dorothy Parker's brief stay in the town was enjoyed by neither of them. Another visitor was Leonard Bernstein, who turned up unannounced one day in Cuernavaca, proposing to move in and stay with her, and bringing with him a grand piano. Martha had admired his looks in Tel Aviv, though she remarked to Walton that he was "reported to like men (also women and goats)," and that he was about as natural as a "20 minute permanent wave" but full of talent and neuroses, "ai, such neuroses." As for any possible relationship between them, it was obvious that he looked on her only as a beautiful placid middle-aged woman, honest as the trees and full of homely wisdom.

Never one to feel easy with visitors staying in her house, Martha moved him smartly into a house up the road, with a large pool, in easy walking distance. He wanted to play Scrabble, which she resisted, hating all games except for gin rummy, but one night, after he had been told by local musicians he met that marijuana made the music flow faster, they got hold of four joints and prepared to experiment. Since they were both terrified of what might happen, they decided to boost their courage by having a few martinis first, generously poured into water tumblers. After a while, beginning to feel ill, Martha crawled toward the spare bedroom. As she reached the bed, she heard Bernstein fall heavily in the sitting room and lie still. She was sick all night; when she fell asleep, her nightmares were appalling. Next morning, she crept reach. Horribly aware of what was happening, conscious, as she had never been before, that it was possible both to love her mother more than anyone in life and yet be driven mad by her presence, Martha pretended that nothing was wrong. Edna concentrated on Sandy. Both longed for the stay to end. When her mother eventually flew back to St. Louis, Martha was seized with anxiety about her mother and fear about her own "deadness." She had behaved, yet again, she said, like a hyena. Nor was this mood of detached boredom only present with her mother. Flavia, too, felt ill-used by Martha. They stopped meeting. Martha told Sybille that she had always feared and hated the weighing out of emotions as if they could be counted, some giving more, some giving less; and that while she always longed for intimacy, when it came, her desire to run for cover was almost uncontrollable.

Alone with Sandy at L'Olgiata, Martha felt her own sense of herself faltering. Nothing was going right. The Topolino was broken into, and two dresses, a suit, and two pairs of shoes that had been made for her were stolen. She was spending more money than she had—over $600 a month—and she was beginning to wonder if she hadn't made a dreadful error in leaving Cuernavaca in such haste. Might they be better off in Trieste? Or in Paris? Could she face another hideously cold winter at L'Olgiata?

Toward the end of the summer, leaving Sandy with his nanny, she had been to meet Sybille on the shores of Lake Maggiore in Switzerland, where she behaved boorishly to their hostess, Esther Murphy Strachey, pointedly going to bed rather than endure the boredom of an evening in her company. Together the two women had made a trip around Switzerland. "My meteoric and impatient friend" was how Sybille described Martha in her account of the journey for *Encounter*. Martha had been delighted by the Swiss, and charmed and entertained by their orderliness and reliability. "What a genius they have for the small change of freedom," she said to Sybille. But she was no more prepared to linger in Switzerland than she lingered anywhere else, and Sybille, who had been journeying in a pleasantly unhurried way before she met Martha, found herself hurtling along the roads in the Topolino. "Let's shove," said Martha, as they sat peacefully on the shores of the lake at Lucerne feeding the swans soon after they met. And so they shoved, up mountains and through valleys, orchards, fields, and woods, down lanes and highways, past castles and lakes, pausing only to eat and sleep.

After they parted, Martha once again took stock of her life. She knew now that she dreaded the idea of going back to live in Rome. The people were all wrong. What she really liked were upper-middle-class intellectuals and artists, and she was fed up with expatriate Americans. They were joyless, and they could not communicate, having been brought up never to admit to doubt, pain, or grief, and they thought failure was dirty, like a nasty disease. Her own next step, on the path to *savoir vivre*—"which will have to do, for me, instead of wisdom"—was not to allow herself to get so depressed and angry when the sky was gray. As for Sandy, and his presence in her life, nothing was said.

Martha called Sybille Bedford "Syb" or "Sybi"; it was her own abbreviation and used only by her. It was Syb who became her closest writing confidante, someone with whom she could pick over not only the act and art of writing but the minutiae of every character and the nuance of every scene. In writing, as in all else, Martha, once engaged, was wholehearted to the point of obsessiveness. For a while, during 1952 and 1953, Syb was her writing partner; there were times when she seemed to be writing for her alone.

At no time in her life was Martha ever more than fleetingly satisfied with anything she had written. As she told Berenson, she felt impelled to write, but it was more like a sentence than a celebration. "Life frays and falls apart," she wrote to him, "and the only way I can make it seem real to me is to write. I never have any time of certainty or self-belief, of feeling that it matters whether I write or polish shoes." She deeply envied those writers who took satisfaction in what they accomplished. Sitting in her study at L'Olgiata, looking out over the cold landscape of winter, hating and resenting the gray skies, yawning and squirming over bilgers that would not flow, and unable to decide whether the Mexican novel should be about her love affair with David or expatriate schemers against McCarthy, Martha felt low. She had made herself believe that it was a failure, a sin, not to love life; joie de vivre, she would say, was one of the *specialités de la maison,* but that was now leaking away. She felt harassed and rather scared. It was Sybille who kept her going, Sybille who comforted her when the "marshmallow paragraph, dripping sentimentality and sweetness,"

made her feel ashamed, and who insisted one day on rescuing a manuscript she had decided to take to the rubbish dump.

Sybille did not find her own writing particularly easy. Her first
book, *The Sudden View,* about Mexico, written in her forties and with
considerable apprehension, would find its English publisher at least in
part through Martha's help. Sybille had sprung upon the world, Martha would tell friends, a quite remarkable writer, disciplined and tal-
ented. She was now at work on a novel called *A Legacy.* Long letters—
sometimes running to seven or eight closely typed pages—went back
and forth between them, as chapters were finished or new ideas sur-
faced, with suggestions for places to expand or cut, ideas for titles and
changes of emphasis. Often, it was a case of shoring up the other's
nerve. "Most people, all people, write as feebly as they speak," wrote
Martha one day. "You write like an angel; angel of another century."
"You must have more confidence," Sybille wrote to Martha. "Yes, I
do know about that flutter in the stomach, one goes quite cold. But
think: you have brought it off before. . . . This one will jell too. Everything you dread most has come off so far (in grinding agony, I admit);
a few weeks ago you thought you could not do the sex. Well, you did
it." Sometimes, Martha complained that Sybille was as protective
about her work as she was about Sandy, "tiger-fierce and basically
frightened."

In their exchanges, Martha could be more brutal than Sybille. Martha was, for instance, obsessed about Sybille's poor spelling and
insisted that she used far too many meals in her fiction. "Bridge party
chapter far too long," came back one message. "Food, food, food. Who
will proofread?" Martha was also far more explosive, and several letters in the thick sheaf of their correspondence are contrite notes from
Martha, apologizing for having erupted uninvited into one of Sybille's
evenings with someone else, and harangued the gathering about the
hell of writing before hurrying away back to L'Olgiata. "I am very
sorry to have behaved, last evening, like a river of pus and gloom,"
reads one. "This unfortunate condition is the usual result of having
spent a day writing with one's feet."

The redeeming factor of Martha's more intemperate and insensitive
outbursts lay, for all her friends, in her humor and great generosity.
One day, realizing how short of money Sybille was while waiting for
a check from a publisher, she sent $200, enough to keep her for three

months. Knowing that Sybille would not accept it from her, she told her that it came from Edna. On the publication day of one of Sybille's books, Martha got a Roman baker to ice a cake with the word *book* spelled incorrectly.

But Sybille was not Martha's only writing confidante. Robert Presnell was becoming another member of Martha's charmed circle of favored men friends. Presnell could be, and was, tough in ways Sybille found hard. "Who is the judge that sits perpetually on your head?" he wrote, in response to a wail of despair. "Write those lines, you silly fool, they are all yours, both the good and the bad, and no one exists in purity and essence. Write the bad lines if only to keep writing. . . . Your ego sits like a fat, repulsive Queen of the Bees, being fed, pampered, caressed. . . . Writing is lonely, wretched, unheralded, often meaningless, insignificant, and too often devoid of even a masturbatory pleasure, mean though that is. Write, Martha, and stop crying at the cold. You've wept long enough."

Martha was not always weeping. Often, she was fuming. Anger against McCarthyism simmered even as she sat writing her bilgers along the Via Cassia. Just as the Jews in Israel had crystallized into figures of gaiety and courage, so those in power in the United States were corrupt and corrupting. How morally right was it for writers, she asked friends guiltily, to lock themselves away?

Early in 1953, she proposed to Mrs. Roosevelt that she should set up a "Citizen's Committee Against Calumny," all of whose members would be sworn noncommunists—their one concession to the "folly of the times being the need to confirm this fact"—and whose job it would be to protect decent, ordinary American liberals from the "deadly rat bites of unsubstantiated individual accusations." Apologizing for burdening her with another chore, Martha added: "I cannot, with comfort, resign myself to the advance of the Dark Ages; so I write to you. Because you are a tower of light, because people will believe you, because you have never been afraid; and because you care about the condition of man, whose only claim to dignity, whose only hope, is the honor of the mind." Martha's faith in Mrs. Roosevelt had not lessened with time, nor had the slightly fulsome tone she now used for her alone.

She had long since realized that for her to use her vehemence effectively, it was no use spreading it too thin. Rage had to be selective.

Nothing gave her more pleasure than meeting Adlai Stevenson, the governor of Illinois, while in Trieste and talking to him about the House Un-American Activities Committee. Before they parted, Stevenson asked Martha to prepare some notes for him to use in his speeches about Americans driven into exile in Italy by McCarthyism at home. When she returned to Rome, she drafted a thirteen-page letter on all the "floating words that make an intellectual and emotional climate." Haunted by a sense of déjà vu, recalling the German refugees from Hitler in the 1930s, she wrote about the fear felt by the Americans she knew in Rome, the way they avoided speaking out because of the fear of having their passports confiscated or being branded "controversial personalities," and the speed with which America's "moral stock" was falling every day. "I think that Orwell and Kafka, in collaboration, are the only writers who could have done justice to this miserable story," she told Stevenson, adding that it would give her great satisfaction to do anything of this kind for him again. It was the start of another good friendship.

Martha had by now left Scribner's and in the summer of 1953 Doubleday in New York brought out the collection of short stories that she had long been working on. Called *The Honeyed Peace,* and dedicated to Sybille and to Winifred Hill, an elderly woman who had befriended her in Cuernavaca, the volume contained stories written as far back as 1937. Many had already appeared in *Harper's* and the *Saturday Evening Post.* If they had a common theme, it lay in the fugitive nature of pleasure or happiness, and many touched on the anguish of readjustment after the clarities of war. One way or another, the characters in all the stories are misfits, misplaced somewhere within themselves. *The Honeyed Peace* includes some of the best short stories Martha ever wrote, like "Venus Ascendant," about a young woman brought to the edge of destruction by a vain and manipulative man. She called it a horror story and said it made her laugh out loud. In "Miami–New York," a somewhat older woman fantasizes about the affair she will have with the young officer seated next to her on her flight home. Many of the characters are lonely women, but the victories they score over their complacent men are not good victories and are sometimes almost unbearably acid. Reviewers were not certain what they felt. Both the *Nation* and the *New York Times* remarked on a new note of desperation in Martha's writing. When the collection of a running debate about the future of Africa, and just where and how the countries that had just gained independence would fit in the modern world, and how blacks and whites would work together. Although her article for the *Atlantic Monthly* has a curiously dated and insensitive ring to it, it has all the hallmarks of Martha's scrupulous honesty. Political correctness was never of any interest to her. "My diagnosis of the quality of Africans is that they lack the time sense," she wrote in the article that appeared nearly a year later, "and so are spared the horror and the nuisance of looking ahead. . . . Their minds certainly do not work as ours do, and facts do not limit and discipline their thinking." She felt extremely guilty, she continued, at the distaste she felt over the way the Africans smelled, but she had been somewhat comforted to find that their own disgust at the white smell, *"l'odeur fade des morts,"* was just as strong. What she did not elaborate on in her article was her contempt for almost all the whites she had encountered. Echoing Paul Scott's words about the whites in India, when he said that it was the work they did that gave them dignity, Martha would talk of her admiration for the professionals, the doctors, farmers, biologists, and teachers, whose skills and dedication gave them substance. In the others, the hangers-on, the wives, those taking and exploiting and giving nothing, she could see no good—and would not bother to look for it.

And there Martha's love affair with Africa might have crystallized, kept alive but not developed further by infrequent visits in search of her lion-colored plains, blue mountains, and vast skies, her heart and spirits lifted by the giraffes and warthogs and dashed by people both white and black, storing up fortitude during spells of solitude, had it not been for an unexpected, and unhappy, turn in her life.

Nine years of marriage; considerably longer, already, than any other of Martha's relationships and, for the most part, companionable, even if she and Tom had always been, and remained, emotionally and temperamentally very different people. Sandy Matthews was now twenty-one, and though Martha continued to berate him for his awful posture, and the stoop that made him look like a "wizened, bent, somewhat ailing gent," she wrote him long and affectionate letters in serious terms on the subjects that interested him. Robust, plain speaking was the tone she continued to adopt with all four of Tom's sons, sometimes apologizing afterward for her hectoring. Gellhorns, she admitted, were noisy and quickly lost their tempers, but they forgot their quarrels just as quickly; the Matthews men, however, were complicated and exhausting, and their facetious tones maddened her. Whether solicited or not, from time to time she fired off letters of admonition and advice that seemed to reflect an increasingly stark view of life. "From observation and experience," she wrote one day to Paul, "I am convinced life is really like going up a mountain slowly and then coming down slowly; but once you start going down, it is just all going down: therefore waste no minutes on the trip up, for they vanish, those minutes, and the hope of them too." After Paul's marriage broke up, in 1961, she wrote that she deplored the welter of self-pity in which he seemed to have sunk. "I wish to shriek a warning: look out before it is too late. . . . The problem is you. The threat to you is pity, coddling . . . bite on the nail . . . swallow it and digest it, and get on with your life, for Christ's sake."

As for her own fat Sandy, there were times when she railed against his greed and laziness, others when she was seduced by his laughter. They quarreled; he lied and was evasive; she grew impatient. During his vacations, some of their best days together were spent bicycling around the English countryside, having set off early from London by train, though Martha continued to fall off whenever she met an obstacle. Sandy, always, was her unprotected flank: second only to Edna, he touched her where she felt most raw.

The routine of her early days with Tom continued. They had acquired a neurotic poodle, Soot, and sent him to an animal psychiatrist, from which he returned to Chester Square fixated on Rosario, terrified of Tom, and believing that Sandy was another poodle. Martha and Tom traveled a great deal: to France and Switzerland; Scandinavia and America; Tangiers, where Martha predictably disliked the Arabs; and Paris, which now repelled her for its attachment to a dead, waxworks past. When the vacation was to be a family outing, Martha would often set out ahead, ferrying their Mini Minor across the Channel and roaming through France alone. She had taken up painting, though even she agreed with Tom that her paintings of people bore an unfortunate resemblance to failed plastic surgery.

The dream of the perfect house remained strong, and one summer, charmed by the white hill villages of southern Spain, with the Atlas

Mountains rising across the sea, she persuaded Tom to let her buy five acres of land between Valencia and Alicante, contributing $18,000 from her own savings. It was to be the first house she had ever built from scratch. There would be a wide terrace with a pergola under which Tom could shelter from the hot sun he hated; and enough heat and solitude for herself. They would grow fruit and vegetables. The plot of land lay in a valley planted with fig trees, up above a rocky riverbed, among "tumbling interlocking green mountains," Martha told Teecher, and the orange groves smelled "like all the weddings in the world." It reminded her of Mexico.

It was not to be. Martha's Spanish house defeated her faster than most of her domestic endeavors. A water diviner was found, and a well dug to a depth of forty meters, but no water flowed. Money trickled away with little signs of activity from the builders. Martha fumed, sitting alone in the half-finished house. "We are foolish. We forget real life," Martha wrote sadly to Alvah Bessie; "22 years of corruption do not improve people: it infects them. . . . Do you remember one of the most beautiful lines of someone or other: 'Hope deferred makest the heart sick'? That's what's the matter, basically, in Spain." After a few frenzied months, exhausted by a kitchen of life made all the more oppressive for being at a distance and in a foreign language, Martha turned her back on her half-built house and fled. Tom, who had never felt much enthusiasm for the project, did nothing more.

Sometime toward the end of the 1950s, trying to resist her constant urge to "rush off to fires," Martha began sifting through her memories and her notes in search of a new idea for a novel. She remembered her Roman life, and the odd assortment of characters who had flocked to postwar Italy, and she thought again about what had happened to her old friend Judy Montagu and her relationship with the American writer Milton Gendel, correspondent in Rome for *Art Review*. Gendel worked for the Olivetti Company, and the wife of one of the Olivettis was his mistress, Vittoria, by whom he had twins. He had been married before, and divorce was not recognized in Italy until almost twenty years later. Judy Montagu, a tall, gawky woman, neither well dressed nor elegant, but very determined, visiting Rome on one of her social sweeps, had fallen much in love with Gendel, an amusing, clever man, whose rather gruff ways were very attractive to women, and pursued him with total, frantic dedication. Eventually, after many scenes, Gendel succumbed. Soon, Vittoria Olivetti was abandoned, and Judy Montagu and Gendel got married, had a daughter, and moved into a magnificent apartment on Rome's pretty central island, where they led increasingly separate lives. In this tale of passion, betrayal, and disillusion, Martha found her material. Making very little attempt to disguise her old friends and acquaintances, beyond casting the story in Paris, and calling Judy "Liz" and Milton "Ben," Martha wrote a short novel about their lives, for once relatively fast and without too much pain. *His Own Man*, she told Bessie, was a "tiny book, very beautifully made, like first class cabinet work" and lighter than a powder puff. The editors at her new house, Simon and Schuster, told her that they liked the book and thought it should be successful. It is in some ways her most entertaining novel, witty, acute, and extremely lively; but it is neither flattering nor kind.

Martha's obtuseness seems to have been casual rather than malicious. In that way that writers find all too easy, she had forgotten about Judy Montagu and the book's origins, and come to see her novel as a book about the seriousness of marriage, in which, as she put it to Teecher, "happiness is not necessarily its aim or product, any more than happiness is the aim or product of life." At least, that is what she later claimed. Judy Montagu did not see it that way. After *His Own Man* appeared in the United States in 1961 to mixed reviews—*Time* magazine complained that the characters wore textiles instead of flesh and blood—Judy Montagu protested to the British publisher, Rupert Hart-Davis, a great friend of her great friend Diana Cooper, and the book was canceled in the United Kingdom. Martha made light of the whole affair and in a statement to her attorneys offered to change at least some of the passages she guessed Judy Montagu had taken offense to. One can see why. Liz, in the book, was domineering, spoiled, a steamroller over the feelings of others, with "a large bust, a hoarse voice, and no one would have said she was beautiful." Liz was also profoundly amoral. Martha said she could easily change "a large bust, a hoarse voice," and that she didn't at all mind altering the wording of a scene in which Liz presses Ben to make love from "This night ought to end in bed" to "This night ought to end in sight-seeing." As for the references to the heroine getting on badly with her dreadful mother, these could be changed to her mother was "too strict." But

Judy Montagu was not mollified, and even Diana Cooper, a friend to them both, could not broker a peaceful solution. (What Vittoria Olivetti made of it all is not recorded, for she wisely kept silent; but her portrait in the book, as Jessica de Camberges, is hardly appealing either: limp and self-effacing to an absurd degree, she manipulates the vain and gullible Ben into fathering her child.) *His Own Man* was not published in Britain, and Judy Montagu did not speak to Martha again. Several mutual friends thought Martha had gone too far.

Something of Martha's occasional deaf ear to the sensitivities of other people was connected, at least partly, to her strong feelings about social life. Nine years of marriage to the gregarious Tom had done nothing to win Martha over to the company of strangers. On the contrary, she felt clearer than ever before that the world was divided between real friends—to whom she was, for the most part, very loyal and devoted—and everyone else, who mattered not at all. Into the category of true friends, who made her laugh and whose language of confidences she spoke and understood, fell Irwin Shaw, Sybille Bedford, Diana Cooper, Lucy Moorehead, Moshe Pearlman, Leonard Bernstein, and a few others. It was, unfortunately, possible to start among the true friends and be cast into darkness, but this was rare; when it happened, Martha could be brutal. Social life, in the sense of dinner parties, the "quark-quark of nattering," Martha loathed in an almost exaggerated way; it took only a few crass or ill-judged remarks to paralyze a dinner table, particularly as Martha had two ways of dealing with acute social boredom: one was to talk, loudly and relentlessly— she said herself that she was prone to turn into a neurotic gramophone to which she listened in horror—and the other was to bolt. There were long evenings of stultifying unease, Tom rather ponderous, Martha tetchy. Letters of Martha's, written to Berenson and his companion, Nicky Mariano, conveyed something of how much she must have hated Tom's easy gregariousness, and how implacable was her distaste for domesticity. October 8, 1955, to Berenson: "Everyone is happy. Except me. I am not happy because I feel like a very old, used, dank, grey rag." (In the Swiss mountains, from which she had just come, she had felt like a "cross between a Valkyrie and a gorilla.") January 14, 1956, to Berenson: "Tom is far happier than I, but then he is not the hausfrau." Eleven days later, again to Berenson: "Ah me. I miss the places, I miss the adored, lost, loony people. I am awfully tired of servant terrible shape," she wrote to Alvah Bessie, "sick from a sense of isolation and desuetude." But she did not give up. In June 1972 she went to Paris to see Madame Nguyen Thi Binh, the National Liberation Front's delegate to the Vietnamese peace conference, to ask her whether she could arrange a visa for the north. She wanted to see for herself the devastation caused by the American bombing around Hanoi, and the *St. Louis-Post Dispatch* had agreed to take a piece. Madame Binh, about whom Martha had earlier written an admiring profile for the *Guardian*'s Women Page, was friendly and, to Martha's surprise, kissed her when they parted. But when the visa came through, it was for a male correspondent, not a woman; the *Post-Dispatch* sent a reporter named Dudman, who, said Martha wearily, knew nothing about Southeast Asia, nothing at all about war, and wrote with his feet. "I have lost hope," she told Betsy Drake, Cary Grant's former wife, and an important new friend in her life. "This is how Women's Lib. was born."

And so she returned to what she could do, which was to work against the war from the sidelines. She wrote to U.S. senators, to friends in government, to the newspapers. Martha, during her lifetime, wrote many letters to newspapers, most of them furious and disbelieving. The dozens she wrote about the war in Vietnam—written and rewritten in many drafts, sometimes by hand, sometimes typed, and all of them scored over and with many crossings out—were among the most outraged. She sent ideas and any new bits of information to writers who were, to her mind, sound on the war, like Anthony Lewis of the *New York Times*. She attended antiwar rallies and demonstrations and joined doctors and priests in trying to raise money to take burned Vietnamese children to the United States for treatment. She scoured the photographs of the bombing and the injured refugees and the occasional harrowing picture of executions and torture with rage and nausea, and wrote to the newspapers about "genocide from the air." She even flew to Washington to take part in Vietnam Moratorium Day. And she continued to write bitter and furious letters to her friends, saying how wretchedly impotent and ashamed she felt to be American, to be a human being, to be alive. "This is so evil and awful, a kind of mad pestilance," she wrote to Sandy Matthews, after the Americans sent B-52s to bomb Quang Tri, where there was a large refugee camp. "If we can't win, we destroy. . . . I am sickened and the helplessness is so awful. . . . I want to be rioting with the students. What else is left except to riot?"

Only contact with people who felt as passionately as she did seemed to assuage her anger, and she exchanged frequent, despairing letters with Senator Fulbright and George Kennan. "We have now parted from every sort of real control over our own policy and over world affairs," replied Kennan to one of Martha's cries of outrage, "and we simply slither and stumble down the precipitate slope of events. Perhaps God will be good to us and we will survive. But it will have to be God, because we have lost control." A world dominated by an America that refused blindly to learn from history, and that was governed by stupidity and immorality: it was all that Martha feared most.

South Dakota senator George McGovern failed to beat Richard Nixon in the presidential elections, and Nixon and his national security advisor and future secretary of state, Henry Kissinger, went on to bomb Cambodia and Laos. Martha referred to Nixon as a "disgusting sick crook" who would go down in history as a "miserable lying murdering little swine." ("Why don't those fucking professors stay at their universities?" she said to a friend about Kissinger.) But the war did finally end. And Daniel Ellsberg, who helped bring about its end after making available to journalists and senators fourteen volumes of mostly classified government documents on the war, became another one of Martha's heroes. "You have earned the respect and gratitude of men of good will everywhere," she wrote to him in an immensely long letter, telling him that his report was "bitter" but necessary homework for everyone.

On January 27, 1973, a peace treaty was at last signed in Paris. It was not so very different from the uncertain settlement made in Geneva nineteen years before, except that over half a million people were dead, and a once densely green and fertile country was pitted, scorched, and littered with debris. The war in Vietnam had lasted longer than any foreign conflict in American history. For Martha, it had indeed been another Spain, but one in which she felt personally complicit; it left, she said, a stone on her heart.

If Vietnam was the stone she couldn't shift, Israel remained Martha's "commitment." In the 1960s, certainly the most political decade of her life, when friends, fiction, travel, Sandy, and even her mother were to some extent pushed out by a grating sense of personal responsibility for the wrong she saw about her, Martha returned again to her own private battle on behalf of the Jews in Israel, a people she saw as traduced by an indifferent and expedient world. There was a danger, she would say, that the Israelis were increasingly seen as military bullies. And just as she wanted to turn the nonpeople of South Vietnam into individuals with hopes and fears, so she wished to show the Israelis as "human," brave, intelligent people, who produced "funny wine and good books, scientists, musicians and farmers of genius."

The trouble, as was so often the case with Martha's most passionately held convictions, was that where there were heroes, there also had to be villains. Injustice demanded perpetrators. Having taken viscerally against the Arabs, she seldom let a chance pass to compare them to the Germans. Gamal Abdel Nasser, who came to power in Egypt in 1957, was the arch villain. He was, she told Bill Walton, "a plain pustullant sore."

Early in the 1960s, long before she thought about going to Vietnam, Martha had decided that she wanted to see for herself what the Palestinians were really like, and asked to visit the UN Relief Works Agency camps in Lebanon, Gaza, and Jordan the *Atlantic Monthly* had agreed to take an article from her. Her mood, from the start, was hostile. "Nothing that I had read or heard prepared me for what I found," she wrote, only this time she intended the words to be ironic. Martha had expected misery, malnutrition, despair; she found, or chose to see, happiness, good health, a people who would have been perfectly willing to adapt to the hand that history had dealt them, were it not for the lies and spirit of hatred fed to them by their leaders. "You all like Nasser?" she reported a conversation in a camp in her notebook. "Smiles. Joy. Certainly do. He will unite us and make us strong. He is our leader. (What a bunch of poor dumb clots. And due to UNRWA— health and schooling, these will be the cream of Arab world). . . . Arab world very stupid. I see no hope for peace. Stupidity rules supreme." In her very long article for the *Atlantic Monthly,* published in the autumn of 1961, Martha heaped praise on the fine parental "care and concern" of UNRWA and warned against Nasser's holy war against Israel and against a 1,000-year Muslim Reich. "The echo of Hitler's voice is heard again in the land," she wrote, "now speaking Arabic."

annoyed when, having been much touched by her delight in the first bottle of scent she professed she had ever seen, she caught sight of a bottle of Chanel No. 5 sitting on her bookshelf. As the days crawled by, she went on admiring her as a writer, and respected her huge courage, but she did not like her. She found her pathetic, ungenerous, and egocentric. "Suffering has not ennobled," she wrote in her notebook. When Mrs. Mandelstam told her that she had been to bed with Osip the first night they met in Kiev in 1919, and that she had not been in love with him then, Martha noted: "I'm beginning to have the sense that all her life since 1938 is atoning for *not* having loved him enough when alive. Mad idea?"

Martha began to count the days, then the hours, to departure. She lay on her bed in her hateful hotel, naked in the stupefying heat, feeling oppressed by Mrs. Mandelstam's hermetic world and infected by her palpable sense of fear. "No papers, no books, radio jammed," she wrote. "No perspective." When Mrs. Mandelstam asked her if she was ever afraid, she replied, "No, only angry." But in her notebook, she wrote: "But not true. I long to escape. The main sensation is pure Big Brother fear." Martha, who was not afraid of death, and had no hesitation about going to a war zone, was very afraid of prison; it was, she said, her one and only real fear, and in Moscow she felt as if she was breathing an air that smelled of secret police. And as the day for her departure approached, she grew increasingly apprehensive that something would happen to keep her a prisoner in the Soviet Union. At the airport, waiting to board her plane, she smoked twelve cigarettes. When the plane took off, she seized on the British Airways magazine and "read avidly," as she wrote later in *Travels with Myself and Another,* "the little booklet that lists all the junky things you can buy on our splendid capitalist airlines." Moscow had been far worse than she could have imagined. Even the people she had expected to like talked a strange dislocated dialogue of nonsequiturs and repeated themselves endlessly, while the drabness and glumness of the city had made it impossible for her to enjoy her usual pastime of observing how the people lived.

After her return to London, Martha and Mrs. Mandelstam kept up their "pen-pallery." "I am keeping the bed and the docs don't know why I have temperature. . . . It is not cancer," Mrs. Mandelstam reported. "But I feel very weak, perhaps it is tedium vitae." Later, she wrote again, though she never dated her letters. "You write that you can't write. You need a war to speak against it. But is it worth having one? I don't think so. . . . But you are not used to thinking and it is time to begin."

Martha felt increasingly out of touch. She suspected that she had been a disappointment to Mrs. Mandelstam, not the acolyte that had been wanted, and that she was too obviously out of sympathy with a closed circle that acted as if it had a monopoly on suffering. Though she redoubled her efforts with publishers and agents on Mrs. Mandelstam's behalf, and sent books and occasional presents of money, she did so largely out of a sense of guilt, and slowly the exchange of letters petered out.

Having hitched her vision of herself so firmly to writing, and having inherited from both parents extremely high standards, Martha effectively created for herself a perilous and demanding world. If to write was her duty, her reason for being alive, then not to write was to fail. To fail as a writer was to fail at life, to be adrift in a formless and uncertain universe with nothing to hold on to. When Martha could not write, when what she called lockjaw of the brain paralyzed her for week after week, or when she read back what she had written and decided it was worthless, she despaired—not only of herself as a writer but as a person, a friend, a human being. She felt herself to be literally pointless and would sit brooding, disconnected, haunted by the futility of the human condition. And, just as when the writing was going well she felt physically strong and healthy, when it went badly she felt ill, "no good way to sit or lie or be, a sensation that the head is slowly swelling and may pop." She got ulcer pains. And with her mother dead, Sandy missing for months at a time, L. affectionate but absent, she had no anchor. All but a very few writers find writing hard; Martha found it excruciating. "I have lost my eye, ear, nerve, and probably am no longer a writer"; this sentence, written to a friend in the early 1980s, was repeated, in a dozen different forms, again and again in letters all her life.

As was her conviction that writers had a duty to discover, and witness, and write; that was their role in life, and it could not be shirked. Even when helpless to change the world, people had no right to the "comfort of ignorance." More than most writers, perhaps, Martha believed not in the determining power of thought but in action: men, as she had told Sandy Matthews, were what they did, not what they thought. Neither Descartes nor Freud appealed to her. If the vision sounded narrow, the black and white uncomfortably stark, the characters in her best short stories do not lack subtlety or nuance. But it was how they behaved, not what they thought, that intrigued Martha. "I cannot analyse," Martha once wrote to Betsy. "It is not my bag." "I consider thinking nearly impossible," she wrote on another occasion. In the sense that she lacked the transforming magic of the true novelist, Martha was not a good writer of fiction; but she was a superb reporter and at her best occupied that fine line where fact ends and fiction begins. She had, as the writer James Cameron once remarked, a "cold eye and a warm heart."

Although Martha was consumed by doubts about her own ability to write, she was absolutely clear about how it had to be done. For a start, you could not both write and live. Writing, she told Sandy Matthews, was "hermit's work," with at the very most another hermit nearby for occasional visits. Four hours a day of actual writing was all that should be attempted, with the rest of the time given to training for the next day. "You need," she wrote, "an absolutely empty outside life if the inside life is to bloom. One has to walk, laze, dream, leave the mind open as a door for the wayward idea and word. The death of writing is engagements." Writing was work, unremitting labor, and no young writer could miss out on a long "self-conducted apprenticeship." All this, of course, presupposed that writers had something that they felt impelled to say.

More important, indeed the single most important factor, was, however, compulsion. You wrote because you had to write, because you had no choice. You wrote because you were angry. "Because," she told Presnell, "one sees, feels and must speak; because one wants to know what one thinks; because it is the hardest work there is and thus, like Everest, it lures . . . something to say which is killing one inside. . . . It gets harder and harder because one knows more, the complexity in the brain is harder to put into words than the violence and clarity of youth; and because one has much better taste and fiercer self criticism. . . . But since there are no happy endings, that is no worse than any other."

And, beyond the discipline, the solitude, and the compulsion, the

the weeks leading up to the event, Martha had decided to give each of her guests a label. Rosie was the "Can-do girl"; Nicholas, "Fortune's favourite kid"; Gillon Aitken, "Power broker." There was a touch of steel in the words she chose, but much thought and much affection had gone into them. Martha used to tell her younger friends that she had outgrown loneliness, insomuch as she had ever known it at all, having been well schooled by Hemingway and Matthews, both of them "positively professors in how to be frozen cold lonely and survive it." But once the chaps entered her life, she was no longer alone.

Martha found getting old extremely hard. Old age was not, as she had hoped, "spiffing"; on the contrary, it was a terrible disease, the worst. She minded, as a woman who had always been looked at, becoming invisible, and she minded even more being seen as old. Two young Frenchmen overtook her one day in the street and looked back, having perhaps been struck by her tall, elegant silhouette. *"Bah. C'est une vieille,"* one said to the other, turning indifferently away. (Martha shouted at them, *"Quels cons."*) When she saw a portrait of herself taken by the photographer Jane Bown, around the time of her eighty-first birthday, she was upset. Who was the especially nice charlady, she asked, this sad, tired, very old woman? She was now closer to Job, she told friends, than anyone she knew.

Martha fought the lines on her face with a face-lift, which she was cross to find so painful and so expensive, and she dealt with the jagged scar left across her stomach by her hysterectomy with more surgery, again painful, to smooth out the tuck. She had an operation to raise her "drooped" eyelids. She was irritated by her "swollen belly and drooping chin." "Find something else to rely on?" she wrote to Betsy. "Like my soul?" She kept up an unremitting assault on her thickening middle by walking determinedly around the Welsh hills with a pedometer strapped to her waist, and she dieted on grapefruit and marmite, and at least once on a new diet pill called Permathene-12. When in London, she went twice a week to a gym to do stretching exercises. It was not just a question of basic discipline, but a public service. And, of course, it worked. Martha, in her seventies and eighties, looked terrific, naturally elegant in very plain clothes often bought from Marks & Spencer or Oxfam, her fair hair well cut, wearing an expression that could be considered haughty except for the humor around her mouth and the irony in her eyes. Her voice, like her vocabulary, was distinctive; droll, wry, self-mocking. It was a bummer stage of life, she said to Betsy. "Everyone grows old. Not everyone grows up. The object is to aim for that, since one cannot avoid growing old."

When she judged her appearance tolerable, and her muscles in good shape, she made dates to meet L., whose distant courtship continued to delight her. She remained very attached to him, appreciative of his niceness to her and of some fundamental quality of honor and innocence that had been lacking in Hemingway and Matthews, though she said of their relationship that it had "such lightness in weight that it would hardly burden an ant."

One summer, fed up with the interminable trudges around the wet Welsh hills, she built a swimming pool at the end of her cottage, a thin glass conservatory twenty-eight feet long and ten feet wide, in which she swam up and down twice a day, setting her alarm clock to go off after forty-five minutes. As an extravagance, she told friends, it could be compared to a yacht. As she swam, with the rain battering on the glass above her head, she listened to Radio 3, saying that she had never cared for opera but that it was not nearly so bad when you could not see the singers, until James Fox taught her how to work a cassette player, and then she listened to Schubert and Chopin and thought about the times she had listened to Chopin during the Spanish civil war. Solitary swimming was dangerous for haunting thoughts, the "coal black mountains" of regret that sometimes tormented her, the "wrong, sad hurting things." She fretted about the harm she might have done to Sandy Gellhorn. She minded never having had a daughter. She wished that she had not wasted ten years on Tom Matthews. "I live with my failures until they choke me," she told Betsy. When the electricity system in the pool failed because of the damp, and the temperature of the water sank below that of a steamy bath, she mended it with her hair dryer. Scorpios were great survivors, she reminded herself and her friends, and indestructible; but they made trouble for themselves, and they were never happy or content except in short bursts.

Martha had always been physically robust, but she was also prone to ill health. As she grew older, she suffered annoying small accidents, perhaps inevitable in someone so restless. She cracked her coccyx slipping on a smooth rock in Gozo, then tore a ligament and wrenched her back in Rome falling down a step onto a stone floor in her hotel bathroom. Her blood pressure sank to that of "a two-toed sloth." She began to suffer from tinnitus, a whine in her ears that sounded like twanging telegraph wires and which destroyed the silence she had sought and loved in Wales. In the late 1970s, she had started getting pains in her back, which were first diagnosed as osteoporosis, "back-bone crumbling . . . bones like a spider's web," and later as a nerve pressing on a disk. Her back grew increasingly troublesome, causing her occasionally to limp and slightly drag her feet, until in 1991 a doctor prescribed anti-inflammatory pills. For a while, she felt better and was able to work on her muscles by more walking and more swimming. But then it grew worse again, and a new doctor gave her slow-release morphine pills, to which she grew briefly unpleasantly addicted. She had become, she said, like her old Honda car, the engine fine and strong, bits and pieces breaking off and falling apart. She thought that she had started to go "briskly downhill" at the age of eighty-two and become "superannuated" at eighty-seven. Even so, in the summer of 1994, she went swimming in three separate seas: the Mediterranean, the Aegean, and the Red Sea.

The solar keratosis on her nose never properly healed, but it was kept under control by repeated courses of radiotherapy and dry ice treatment. Her old ear infection, dormant for many years, flared up again whenever she swam too long in the sea. Small skin cancers had to be burned off her face. Worse, considerably worse than any of this, however, was the slow reduction of sight. All through the 1980s, Martha had been conscious of a problem with her eyes. In the spring of 1991, she was told that she would need a cataract operation on one eye. For the first two weeks after leaving the hospital, she was elated: her earlier excellent vision seemed to have been restored, in that eye at least. But then her sight began to fail. For a while, Martha raged against the eye surgeon, insisting that he had botched the operation. But then it became clear that she was in fact suffering from macular degeneration, an irreversible condition involving central vision. It meant that reading became first hard, then difficult without the strongest magnifying glass, and finally all but impossible. She was told that she would never go blind, but her right eye could soon detect very little.

To her younger friends, Martha treated her ailments lightly. She made jokes with John Hatt about having to ask strangers whether she

ACKNOWLEDGMENTS

IN THE SUMMER of 1969 I was pregnant with my first child. My husband, Jeremy, and I came to London from Rome, where we were living, to wait for her birth. There was a heat wave, day after day of the sort of weather I now know Martha Gellhorn most liked. One evening, she asked us to dinner. I wish I could remember what we talked about, but I do remember how, as we left the restaurant, I realized that the baby was coming. Early next afternoon my daughter was born. We called her Martha. My mother's name was also Martha, though she was always known as Lucy, and the two women were very good friends. The omens seemed right. Two reflective, funny, clever women; Martha was bolder; my mother more loving. They had a lot of fun. The name seemed a good start for a child.

I was never one of Martha Gellhorn's "chaps," the close circle of younger friends, women as well as men, who gathered around her in the last twenty years of her life. I was always a little frightened of her. But there was never a time when she was not somewhere in my life, as my mother's friend, someone to hear about, and laugh with, and admire. Like the many people who talked to me for this book, I miss her slightly drawling, self-mocking voice, her ironic glance, her certainty that misfortune can and must be handled with fortitude and dignity and that it is we who owe the world a duty, and never the world that owes us anything. To fight, to keep going, to be compassionate; whenever possible, to laugh—that, for me, was Martha's message. Often, of course, she failed, as we all do. She could be dismissive, imperious, insensitive, and even cruel. But she tried, and she did not complain; that is what I remember.

I would most particularly like to thank Alfred Gellhorn, Martha's youngest brother, for his constant help, encouragement, and friendship, as well as Sandy Gellhorn, her adopted son, and Sandy Matthews, her stepson and literary executor, and his wife, Shirlee, for all their advice, reminiscences, and hospitality. I am extremely grateful for the access Sandy Matthews kindly gave me to Martha's papers and for permission to quote from her letters, diaries, and unpublished works.

Howard Gotlieb, the director of the Department of Special Collections at Boston University, where Martha's archive is lodged, was immensely helpful during my visits to the library, as were his archivists, Sean Noel and Nathaniel Parks. I could not have written this book without their help. I would like to thank them very much. Margaret Rich and AnnaLee Pauls of the Special Collections Library at Princeton University very kindly took the time and trouble to track down a series of letters for me, as did Steven Plotkin and James Roth at the John F. Kennedy Library in Boston; I am most grateful to them all. I also consulted archives and papers in the British Library; the London Library; the Eton College Library; the Seeley G. Mudd Manuscript Library in Princeton; the Beinecke Rare Book and Manuscript Library at Yale University; the Manuscripts and Archives Division, and the Berg Collection, of the New York Public Library; the Franklin D. Roosevelt Library in Hyde Park, New York; the State Historical Library of Wisconsin; the University of Oregon; the Rare Book and Manuscript Library of Columbia University, New York; the University of South Carolina; the Ohio State University; the Harry Ransom Humanities Research Center at the University of Texas at Austin; the Library of Congress; the Bancroft Library at the University of California; the College of Physicians of Philadelphia Library; the George Arents Research Library, Bird Library, Syracuse University; Radcliffe College; the University of Louisville; the Rare Book and Special Collections Library at the University of Illinois at Urbana-Champaign; the Special Collections at the Washington University Libraries; and the Harvard University Center for Italian Renaissance Studies at I Tatti in Florence. I would like to thank their staffs and archivists for their help in locating relevant material.

For their memories of Martha, and for lending me letters and giving me permission to quote from them, I would particularly like to thank: Gillon Aitken, David Albert, Sybille Bedford, Anna Benn, Jane Bernstein, Dora Block, Mary Blume, Rosie Boycott, Bill Buford, Cornell Capa, Harriet Crawley, Betsy Drake, Nikki Dobrski, Lady Pamela Egremont, Gloria Emerson, Horst Faas, George Feifer, James Fox, Peter Gellhorn, Flavia della Gherardesca, Victoria Glendinning, Rob and Loraine Grover, Shusha Guppy, Jerry Hannifin, Clarice Incisa, Jeremy Harding, John Hatt, Clare Hollingworth, Sue Hoyle, Jenny Hughes, Ian Jack, Hugues de Jouvenel, Ward Just, Cynthia Kee, Phillip Knightley, John P. Matthews, Pamela Matthews, Paul Matthews, Jeffrey Meyers, Patricia Milbourne, Pauline Neville, John Owen, Agi Paoloczi-Hovarth, David Pearlman, Bernard Perlin, Sir Edward Pickering, John Pilger, Marsha Presnell, Ruth and Sol Rabb, John Randal, Marilyn Sale, Ann Sebba, Amanda Shakespeare, Nicholas Shakespeare, Adam Shaw, John Simpson, Elsie Smith, Jon Snow, Natasha Spender, Peter Straus, Hugh Thomas, Raleigh Trevelyan, Peter Viertel, Vicky Weston, Richard Whelan, Milton Wolff, and Barry Zorthian.

In St. Louis, four friends of Martha's helped me to reconstruct her early days: Virginia Deutch, William Polk, the late Archer O'Reilly, and Mary Taussig Hall. I am very grateful to them. Also in St. Louis, the staff of the John Burroughs School found copies of Martha's early writings for me in the school review and told me about the school's creation, the archivists at the *St. Louis Post-Dispatch* produced her first articles, and the Saint Louis Public Library and the Western Historical Manuscript Library at the University of Missouri in St. Louis unearthed material relating to her life and family. Mrs. Coralee Paul did some research for me in and around the city. In Florence, the archivists at the Harvard University Center let me consult the correspondence between Martha and Bernard Berenson. I am grateful to them all.

I would also particularly like to thank the following people for their hospitality and help during the months of my research: Jill Kneerim, William Bell, and Lexie Eliot in Boston; Jane Kramer and Vincent Crapanzano in New York; Helen Wilmerding in Princeton; and Lyndall Passerini in Cortona. My son, Daniel Swift, did some research for me in New York. My warm thanks go to my editor at Chatto & Windus, Penny Hoare, my editors at Henry Holt, Ileene Smith and Jennifer Barth, and to my agent, Clare Alexander. As always, I am particularly grateful to Anne Davie, Teddy Hodgkin, and Julian Schuckburgh, for reading the manuscript and making many helpful suggestions.

INDEX